About the Author

Elizabeth Hedley was born in Darlington in 1926 and now lives in Freshwater Bay on the Isle of Wight, not far from the Needles Radar Station where she was a Radar Operator. She and her husband Richard Hutchings returned from New Zealand in 1961 with their three Kiwi sons, Keith, Nigel and Simon. 2016 sees the celebration of thirty years of their Hunnyhill Publications. They had a bookshop in Shanklin and Winchfield Gardens in Newchurch. Elizabeth was the organizer of the pioneering Isle of Wight Social Services Home Sitting Service supporting carers. Elizabeth spent 30 years in Broadclyst creating her organic garden and now lives in Freshwater Bay with her son Simon.

Other books by the Author

Gardening for Lily - The Story of an Organic Garden
and it's Family

Discovering the Sculptures of George Frederick Watts
O.M., R.A.

Discovering Isle of Wight Sculptures

Busts & Titbits - Woolner Busts & Freshwater
Fragments

Dedicated to Richard and to Keith, Nigel and Simon and
their families

Elizabeth Hutchings

YOUNG WAAF
HITCH-HIKER'S
GUIDE TO ENGLAND

AUSTIN MACAULEY
PUBLISHERS LTD.

A CIP catalogue record for this title is available from the British Library.

ISBN 9781786129758 (Paperback)
ISBN 9781786129765 (Hardback)
ISBN 9781786129772 (E-Book)
www.austinmacauley.com

First Published (2017)
Austin Macauley Publishers Ltd.
25 Canada Square
Canary Wharf
London
E14 5LQ

Acknowledgments

I wish to acknowledge the help and support of my family and my many friends worldwide. They all know who they are and many know each other through the wonderful internet.

Book 1

Introduction

On looking back through these two books I find myself remembering people, places and incidents which have come into my life which I would otherwise have forgotten completely.

This was the real life for me when I was in the W.A.A.F. [W.R.A.F. since February 1949, thus reverting to its original title in WW1] Every moment that I was seeing England by hitch-hiking I felt really alive and free. I'm very glad indeed that I have kept these records and only wish for two things concerning them. Firstly, that I had taken photographs all along the way and secondly that I had had the real talent for description so that I could record everything. I fear I have left gaps, too, that my few notes will never quite be able to fill in.

I would have liked to share all my pleasure with others, but I think that only to me will the following pages ever be adequately alive to be interesting.

I have all my maps as well, which I love to look at and study. The names stir up vivid memories also, so that with books and maps I can delve into the past and go through any one of these experiences again in my mind if not in actual fact.

November 21, 1949

Nigel encouraged me to start my *ELIZABETH – A QUARTET* in 2004 and once again with his encouragement I have today started recording these two books which have 61 hitch-hikes starting on July 21 1945 from Ventnor to Beer in Devon. Those Bartholmew maps formed the 'wallpaper' in our bedroom in our first New Zealand home in 1951, our dairy farm at Tokoroa in the Waikato.

On VE Day, May 8 1945 I was on leave at home, Elton Cottage in Hook in Hampshire and received a telegram from the Needles radar station informing me that they were closed and I could stay on leave until they found somewhere for me to be posted. In the event, I went to the radar station at Ventnor. On January 6, 1946, some the men from the men's camp along the road in Upper Ventnor came to our WAAF camp asking us to go swimming. Several of us went directly down to the beach by the various steps. It was extremely cold but we were soon warm after we had climbed back up.

November 23, 2015

I

Ventnor to beer in Devon

On July 21 1945 I was unable to be off duty until 1230. I was rushed to catch the bus to Newport, but fortunately it was late. From Newport I got a lift with a man in a private car for almost 2 miles. Then I signalled a huge civvie lorry, which took me to Yarmouth. It was going on to London but that did not help me this time.

The boat across to Lymington was packed with roughly 20 cars. Most of them, returning holidaymakers were full of luggage and children. At Lymington I was almost first out of the boat and took up my stand where all the cars would pass me. The second car appeared to be full, so I did not signal it but it stopped and I got in. It was half-full of luggage, the other half was occupied by the wife and 15-month-old daughter of the driver and the little girl sat on my knee. They were heading for Salisbury so took me to Cadnam.

It was not long before a man in a private car stopped in answer to my signal. He was on his way from Coventry to Wareham. I was the fourth service person he had helped. He put me down at the turning to Wareham just beyond Poole, called Lytchett Minster. It was about quarter of an hour before a family picked me up and took me to Bere Regis. I'm still puzzled as to where Bere acquired its Regis. One day I must find out. [Edward, I made it into a Free Borough hence the Regis? 2015]

Then I got a lift in quite a large car with two men in front and an AC in the back. They were going to Taunton but the AC got out of the small turning just this end of Dorchester. They took into the top of the town and from there I walked out of the town towards Bridport.

My next lift I signalled before I realised that it was already full. The car was very old and dilapidated and an old man was driving, with three women. The one in front went and sat behind and I'm sure they must all have been uncomfortable, but they insisted on giving me a lift. That incident reminds me of what has happened to me so often and what many people I have met have told me. People who obviously have heaps of room do not stop but those whom it will inconvenience do their utmost to help you. This does not apply always and I must admit that most people I meet while hitching have been extremely kind.

They put it down about 8 miles out Dorchester where the road turns off to the left down to Long Bredy. The views southwards from there was lovely and typically Dorset. In the distance were grassy hills, one was covered by a low-lying cloud of mist, and a valley came right up where I was standing. To the left near a few scattered houses, nestled in the valley was a large house well in keeping with its surroundings. The size and beauty of this house was similar to those of a house of which I had only caught a glimpse on the other side of Dorchester. It was three-part surrounded by hills but I saw it from its open side up a long valley with an avenue trees either side. I hope later on in this book to be able to record having been through this beautiful County of Dorset with more time to spare for its hills and valleys, for its country towns and quaint hidden away hamlets and villages and for the lovely cliffs on the South Coast of which I have only been told and have not seen as yet.

It was with this pleasant scene on either side of me, but with the mist quickly coming down to blot it out that I got a truly providential lift. A smallish car drew up beside me. I hadn't signalled as it appeared to be full. Inside was an attractive girl with Flt Lieut. They pushed aside some of the suitcases in the back and said, 'Yes', to my enquiry about taking me to Bridport. Then came my surprise when I opened the door the whole the interior of the car was covered with confetti. I was very grateful to them for giving me a lift and had every intention of getting out at Bridport. Then the girl asked where I was heading and I replied, 'Well, I don't expect you know it, it's a little place in Devon called Beer.' At this they both laughed and said that that was where they were going for their honeymoon!

At Bridport they wanted to stop for something to eat but as it was already 6.30 we were unable to find anywhere open. They gave me some very nice sandwiches and meat pasties, which they said they were to full to eat. Their aim and object really was a cup of tea. Coming down into Charmouth the scene once more was lovely. The village lies in a valley which runs straight down to the sea. I had never seen it from the east before but several times while cycling down the other way I have seen the whole valley completely filled with huge white feathery clouds or bathing in the sun.

In Charmouth we stopped for a drink before climbing out of the Valley on the other side and so on to Lyme Regis. Still keeping to the coast road we climbed up to Rousden and passed Allhallows School where in the winter of 1941-1942 I used to cycle from St Mary's to play hockey. Up on the top once more we branched down to the left by one of the shortcuts in among the hills and trees which I found so much nicer when I used to bicycle round these parts from Beer. Down at the bottom we came to Axmouth, that quaint little village just before Seaton and on the opposite side of the Axe. The sea again at last. How I have learned during the war to love being near the sea. I doubt if I will ever be able to settle down very far from it again. * I do not like Seaton as it is such as a straggling and flat town. The winds sweep up from the sea and it seems to have none of nature's usual protection. So often the River Axe looks ugly too when at low tide so very little water is left and her bare, brown bed is left exposed and empty.

From Seaton we got the first glimpse of the picturesque cliffs on its western side, which seclude Beer entirely between them. I think Beer is one of the very best situated villages I have seen. You don't even know of its existence until you come upon from the road behind. From either side, east and west, it is as if the cliffs continue without a break. Thus I arrived at Beer for the last time while we were living there. I shall almost certainly be returning. Never again will it be home for me.

I shall always have very happy memories both of Beer and its people and the lovely surrounding Devonshire coastland. *2015 living two hundred yards from Freshwater Bay.

II

Beer to Yarmouth

After a pleasant and quiet weekend, here after my four
and a quarter hour journey on the Saturday from
Lymington once again I set out on my travels. This time
the journey, which I was compelled to do though I would
much rather have stayed at Beer. But the Air Force do and
I had to be Ventnor by Tuesday 13.00 hours. My intention
was to bus to Axminster to get onto a more main road.
When I got to Seaton I had about half an hour's wait until
13.00 hours so I stopped a car in the hopes and they took
me to Axmouth, where I could get a hitch more easily but
where the bus would catch me up if I was unfortunate.
After almost a quarter of an hour I signalled a large car
which I discovered was a taxi. There was a very nice
couple in the back who are only too willing to take me to
Axminster where they were catching the train by which I
should really have been travelling. Just outside the station,
I got another lift with a civvie in a private car up to
Hunters Lodge. The road goes uphill but towards
Charmouth. I know it well from previous days with my
great-uncle at St Mary's [Uplyme] close by.

It was nearly half an hour before I got a lift to Monkton [?]. The owner of the car was most awfully kind and took me a mile or so further on so it only left couple of miles should I have to walk into Charmouth. The rest of the road is deeply cut and runs down the valley. Only a few minutes passed before a couple in a small green car picked me up and took it down to Charmouth. They didn't know the way to the beach so I was able to help them in return for their kindness to me. So often I have been able to help people when they have given me lift. This incident reminds me of when I went from Hook to Lyndhurst with an extremely nice Dutchman, who was on his way from London to Bournemouth, but had read the book wrong and thought it was only 56 miles! Also he didn't know the way so when I got in he didn't have to keep looking at his map.

But I am so busy reminiscing that I've completely left behind Charmouth and my endeavours to get back to Lymington in time for the last boat 19.15 hours. I crossed the little bridge at the bottom of the main street and took up my stand once more. This time I had hardly any time to wait. A large, highly polished black car came down the street. It stopped when I signalled. The driver was a woman and there were two women in the back. The latter were being taken to Dorchester, evidently for shopping. This was an absolute gift as it got me well on my way and also on the main road. I always find it an advantage to have a town behind me when hitching as naturally more cars come from there than from the small villages. I sat in the front and was in the height of luxury all the way. The fourteen-horsepower purred along and the occupants were very interested when I told them of my intention to get to the Isle of Wight by the evening and of my previous journey on the Saturday. Dorchester seemed to be a nice town but I did not stop to explore it. I soon got a lift to a turning about 2 miles out. After a few minutes a man stopped in his car and said he was going to Poole. On the way we turned off to the left and I waited in the car about 10 minutes while he did some business with the grocer at Puddletown. He told me he worked for a firm which dealt with tinned foodstuff. They supply Laceys and Orchards with whom my landlady in Freshwater deals and also Dearloves in Hook. Further on we stopped at Bryants Puddle where he did similar business with the village shop. The signpost here directed people to Affpuddle and Tolpuddle. [Famous for the Martyrs] What an amazing name some places do get. I must try and find out the origin of these Puddles. [2015. In the valley of the River Piddle. Domesday Book – Affpuddle Affapidela. Briantspuddle owned by the Frampton Family who sold it to Ernest, later Sir, Debenham son of the founder of Debenhams. For the full fascinating story Google Briantspuddle]

At Poole I left the car and soon got a lift with an RAMC Major and a VAD. This was a very bad mistake as they were only going to Bournemouth. If only I had realised I would have waited for a lift that would take me all the way through. We live and learn! I must remember next time I go that way.

My impressions of Bournemouth were very favourable. The town is clean and big and one of the nicest through which I have ever been. I got a trolley bus

21

out to Christchurch. Incidentally I only just got the bus and nearly slipped off as it was already moving when I saw it. It was a silly thing to do but, 'All's well that ends well'.

I was still in Christchurch when a man pulled up in his car and asked if I wanted to go to some place of which I had never heard but he said it was on the way to Lyndhurst, my next objective, So I got in. He had only been out of the RAF 16 days and was feeling very pleased with life. He had just got his car on the road again and that also pleased him, which he showed by the speed at which he drove. I told him I had taken half an hour to get out of Bournemouth and I was on my way to Lymington. At this he told me In very superior tones that I should not rely on transport such as buses but that I ought to hitch. Naturally he was most surprised when I told him that I had hitched to Beer on Saturday and was just on my way back.

That reminds me of an incident on the Isle of Wight when several people including myself were left behind by the Newport bus at Whitley Bank. As a car came along they all began telling me that if I stood in the road and put out my hand they should give me a lift. 'Being in the Services'. They wanted me to signal the car just as it came round the corner about four or five hundred yards away. I had never been instructed in the art of hitching by civilian housewives and holiday makers before and it really amused me.

I was dropped at an aerodrome and very soon a large army lorry picked me up. The driver was on his way back to London having driven down to Bournemouth in the morning. He intended staying the night in Southampton on his return journey. At Lyndhurst a civilian stopped his car and took me to within a couple of miles of Lymington. I think he had probably just been demobbed. Anyway he had quite recently come over from Belgium. I should think he was probably a Major or perhaps an RAF officer.

Very soon afterwards a civilian who lived in Lymington took me down to the bottom of the town. When I got to the station I found I was 20 minutes late for the 17.40 boat so I had to wait until a quarter past seven. I satisfied thirst and hunger with an orange and so ended my journey of over a hundred miles on the Lymington Yarmouth ferry. I really enjoyed my weekend and the weather was kind to me all the time.

III

Lymington to Hook

Before Monday, July 30, 1945 I had hitched this particular journey several times, including the return from Hook to Southampton or Lymington. In a previous chapter I mentioned being fortunate in getting a lift right from Hook to Lyndhurst. On another occasion, June 2 I left Yarmouth by the eight thirty boat and was in Hook by eleven thirty. I left just before midday and got a lift with a naval officer, who was already giving a lift to an Army private. It was from him that I learned a useful piece of information. We passed several small lorries and he said they were going to Southampton and did so every day about that time. I had to get out at the turning to Salisbury and the officer got out too and when the first lorry came along he stopped it for me and asked if they would take me. I was thus in Southampton by one o'clock.

This time I crossed over to Lymington by the one twenty boat but unfortunately it was late leaving. There was a light Army transport on board and the ATS girl driving it gave me a lift to the first turning along the Winchester bypass, which got me well on the way. My next lift took me to the turning to Alton. It was not far but I was not quite certain when I accepted the lift where the turning was. The occupants were an ATS officer and her driver. I seemed to be fated to have Army lifts that day. A minute little car came along very soon and when it stopped the Captain inside said he was going to Hook, which of course was just what I wanted. On the way I discovered that he had been stationed in Hook for two years and knew quite a lot of our friends. I was surprised to see that he knew the South so well as I had difficulty in understanding his broad Scottish accent. I was home by four o'clock which was very nice as I only had that night before returning to Ventnor.

IV

Hook to Southampton

On the morning following my journey from Lymington to Hook I had to wend my way back in time for duty at one o'clock at Ventnor, where I was then stationed. This meant getting up early but it would have been even earlier if I'd gone by train. At about twenty past seven I got a milk lorry at Hook, which took me to the Basingstoke bypass. He had been travelling since two o'clock and said he did the journey every morning and then back again. It was not very long before a private car stopped, when I put my hand out. The occupants were a family on the way from somewhere in Buckinghamshire to Highcliffe. They were going on holiday and had started at half past five in the morning. It was certainly a lovely morning for motoring. Unfortunately, I didn't know exactly where Highcliffe was. We went along the Winchester bypass and a few miles beyond the Southampton end of it they saw a turning which said Romsey so they dropped me and said that was the best way. My next lift, after a wait of about a quarter of an hour was in a private car with a man who told me that it would have been much better for them to have gone right down to Southampton. It was a pity but nothing could have been done about it then. This car dropped me at the top of Southampton and I was able to get a tram right down to the Royal Pier where I arrived at nine o'clock, with half an hour to spare before the ferry went over to Cowes.

V

Newport to London

Thursday, August 2 was the first day of my leave. I was able to get off early and got a bus from Ventnor into Newport. From there the only way of getting the boat at Yarmouth was to hitch. The main difficulty with Newport, as with so many towns is to get out onto a main road from where one can begin to hitch. There was a policeman directing traffic in the middle of the town and he asked me where I wanted to go, when he saw that I was trying to get a lift. I told him and the second car he stopped was a private one and the owner took me all the way to Yarmouth. Just as I got there the one twenty ferry was just leaving. It was annoying to miss it but I was only trying to catch the three o'clock one so it was not so bad. I had a long wait in Yarmouth but when I got to Lymington an Army Captain gave me a lift to Lyndhurst. I was much too late for the train at Brockenhurst so that my only chance was to hitch. My aim and object was to be in London to meet my sister-in-law [my brother, John's wife Kay] and niece with whom I was travelling up to Scotland by the night train.

From Lyndhurst I got a lift to Chandlers Ford with a commercial traveller. I don't know why but I never seem to be very good at getting lifts at that particular spot. It must have been about twenty minutes before I got a lift in a private car to the Southampton end of the Winchester bypass. The lorry that then picked me up was going to Kings Worthy. I did not know then where that was but I was soon to find out. It was at the opposite end of the bypass. On the corner there was an airman who very soon got a lift in rather a slow moving lorry. A few cars passed me and then a nice looking private one stopped. Just as I was getting into the front seat another car pulled up and a Flying Officer got out. We waited for him and he said he also was going to London. The driver said he was going to Hartley Wintney, and off we went at an average speed of 50 M.P.H. Just as we were going along the Basingstoke bypass he told us that he was trying to catch up with a friend of his who had left Christchurch, just ahead of him but who was going all the way to London.

At the little black café just beyond Hook he suddenly pulled up and turned in. There was his friend, just ordering a cup of tea. We all joined in and just after six o'clock we got into the other car. I was most surprised when, just before Camberley we went right through a huge aerodrome. I had not been along that road since before the war and of course it was a great difference. [2016. This would have been Blackbush from where, after the war my new sister-in-law Pam Hutchings would fly as an airhostess and by chance met Richard and me at Nice Airport both on our cycling journey to and from Rome.

On the second encounter she allowed us into her hotel room for much-needed and most welcome baths.]

At Staines, we got a puncture but with the owner taking off the wheel and the officer and myself getting out the spare wheel it was only about 5 minutes before we were on our way again. The officer was on his way to Birmingham I think it was and only had a few days in England. He had not been back from India for several years and even this was only a duty trip which seemed rather hard after so long away.

I'd only been along that road once before and that was a long time ago. I think it's a very nice road and the scenery is simply lovely. We were taken to Holland Park tube station and from there it was only about ten minutes before I was in King's Cross and waiting in the queue for the train with Rosemary insisting on being carried and trying to wear my awful WAAF hat. I only wished I could have hitched all the way to Scotland as I do hate train travelling even if it is a bit more certain. [Rosemary was John and Kay's daughter born on July 13 1943 while he was in Africa with the Royal Marines.]

VI

London to Southampton

On August 11 I arrived in London by train from Berwick. On my way by tube from King's Cross I stopped at Marble Arch and went to see if the rumours about the war being over were really true. Oxford Street was littered with paper but still the headlines of the newspapers were telling of delays in peace negotiations. Anyway I had seven o'clock breakfast at Lyons and then by tube and bus I arrived on the Staines road. After only a few minutes to wait I got a lift in a small private car with a Scotsman, though I had only just come down from Scotland I had some difficulty in understanding him. As he was going to Basingstoke it was a very useful lift for me as I was only going to Hook that Saturday and going on to Southampton on the Monday.

After a lovely weekend at home I set off on Monday afternoon at two o'clock. My first lift was in quite a big car with three men and a boy. The two in the back moved up to make room for me. They took me beyond Basingstoke to the turning to Salisbury. Not long after they left a small private car stopped. There was a married couple in front and they moved all their belongings up into one corner at the back and in I got. They said they could help me some of the way to Southampton. It turned out in the end that they were going all the way there. At Kings Worthy, they did not go to the left down the bypass but straight on to Winchester. They informed me that it was much quicker. This I certainly agreed with when we got to the other end but it is still a very good bypass [I remember it being built just before the war but in 1994 it was dug up and reverted to countryside when the St Catherine's Hill section of the M3 opened. 2016] and most necessary as the Winchester streets are not made for heavy lorries and the amount of heavy traffic which is bound to pass that way.

When we got to Southampton I was in good time for the ferry and we went down to the Royal Pier and from the road we were able to see the Queen Mary. Later, on the ferry I got a much better view. She certainly is a magnificent sight and must look wonderful at sea. [Was she indeed the hospital ship lit up in the Solent which I had plotted and then seen early in 1945? In 1950 Richard and I would meet her every time she returned from New York to deliver her plants and flowers from Dogmersfield market garden where we were working until our epic journey by bikes and boats to New Zealand]

On the Wednesday I was once more home having gone up by train on Monday night as I was not needed at Ventnor. This Wednesday was August 15th, a date that will be remembered for ever as it was with a light heart that I set off, with the knowledge of Peace at last. At about seven fifteen in the morning I once again got the milk lorry, which I have mentioned previously in this book. Chapter 4. I had a few minutes wait at Basingstoke on the bypass, which was unfortunate as it was pouring with rain. Soon a lorry pulled up and I got in. I got on the cylinder between the driver and his passenger. The rain was even coming in there but it was better than being outside and stationary. They left me at the Salisbury turning just beyond 'The Wheatsheaf'. There I did not have long to wait before another lorry came along. In this lorry I got all the way to Southampton once again going right through Winchester. This time it was because the driver was delivering weekly newspapers and so we stopped at a small shop before we continued.

The conclusion to all this was that I missed the nine thirty ferry just because I didn't bother to get the first possible tram to the pier. Anyway I learned my lesson, as I had to wait a long time for the next boat.

VII

Weston Zoyland to Hook

On August 25th, a Saturday I had a good journey home from Somerset. On the previous Tuesday I was posted (a habit of the Air Force) to a place previously unknown to me, called Weston Zoyland. I'm afraid my first impressions were not favourable and now that I am at last safely away I look back with distaste at the place. Anyway, I determined to get away every week possible and it being my birthday on the Monday I decided to go home. When I made enquiries as to which was my best way everyone seemed to have different ideas. Some said get to Bristol, others to Bath and a few said, 'go down to Taunton or even to Glastonbury.' I have since found from experience that the Bristol idea is really the best. From Weston Zoyland I got a lift in the sidecar of the sports NCO though at the time I had no idea who it was. It seemed that I was standing on the Bath Road for a very long time before a car stopped. They were only going a few miles but as I had to take the plunge sometime I decided to go. Then another car took me a few more miles. Then in a few moments my luck changed. A small car came tearing along and although I signalled it, it was obviously not going to stop then suddenly it pulled up. I opened the door and the driver said 'Hullo Elizabeth what are you doing here?' The coincidence was amazing. It was one of the men from Ventnor. He was on leave and had been since before I was posted, so he had no idea I was no longer there. I confess I could not remember his name, in fact I do not think I had heard it before. Anyway he informed me that his name was Bernard and he introduced me to his friend Bill. By this time we were on the way and I had discovered to my delight that they were going to High Wycombe, which meant they could drop me in Reading. I would like to emphasise the luck and coincidence of this lift as I would certainly not advise anyone to take this route in the normal way, as the traffic is not at all good. We stopped at... and had a drink. Then when we got to Devizes we went to the Cheese Cake Café where we had an excellent tea, with salad and lovely little cakes. Bill seized the opportunity to buy a present for his son and so on to Reading. There they left me and unfortunately, I have not met either of them since.

It was some time before I got a lift in a big car to just outside Reading. Then I foolishly turned down an offer of a lift to Hartley Whitney. The next car took me to Basingstoke and from there I got a lift in a private car to Hook with a family on their way to London from Bournemouth. I'm afraid I was rather late in getting home but that was due to our stopping for tea and I enjoyed the day so much that it really did not matter. When I got home it was to find a lovely birthday cake made by my mother and she had also made me a lovely handbag, which made the perfect end to a perfect day.

VIII

Weston Zoyland to Lymington

On the weekend following my trip home by Reading one
of the WAAF in the section and myself got the offer of a
lift in the Sergeant's car. He was going down to Fareham
and I wanted to get to Lymington as I was once more
visiting the Isle of Wight. Pam wanted to get to London.
Sarg had only just bought his Singer so we all prayed that
it would not break down and leave us stranded. For the
first few miles it kept stopping but in the end it seemed to
be going all right. We went out through the back of the
camp to Middlezoy and eventually joined the main road,
passing through Wincanton. I think it must have been just
beyond the Mere that we encountered a hill that the car
simply refused to take. By now it was pouring with rain,
which did not help matters. We had started off at one
fifteen instead of twelve o'clock so by now we have lost a
lot of time. After several attempts the car backed into the
side of the road and got entangled in some barbed wire.
When we got out of this mess. Pam and I decided to try
another lift as time was getting on. The first thing that
stopped was a private car that was full and could be of no

assistance. Then a Royal Marine truck stopped. Pam and I got in, loathe to leave Sarg alone with his car but it was no use quibbling about that when we had to get on. The last boat over to the Island is seven o'clock. The Marines dropped us at a corner on one of the main roads to Salisbury, within about ten miles of the town. It was still raining I'm afraid and Pam was getting most disgruntled. I said she'd better take the first lift that came along which of course was only going to Salisbury, where, I heard later she got a train. I fear her faith in hitching was very shaken but then one needs to be very self-confident and optimistic and always keep up one's spirit when hitching. The next car was going to London by Amesbury so was of no help. By this time I had been waiting ages. An American jeep had picked up a GI, but had ignored us. While Pam and I were at the corner by a garage a private car came from the Wincanton direction and the driver came over and asked us the way to somewhere we had never heard of. The next thing we knew was that the car was alight under the front passenger seat and the three occupants were getting out. Fortunately there was someone at the garage who helped them and on they went. At last a private car drew up and a very nice couple said they could take me to Salisbury. I told them of my determination to get to Lymington so instead of stopping as they had intended, for tea in Salisbury they continued on their way to Bournemouth.

Then I did another silly thing, but we live and learn. I got out at Ringwood hoping to get to Cadnam but there was no hope so I went to the station to find the Lymington train had just left. I was exasperated but my luck changed again as I came out of the station a huge car pulled up for two soldiers. I said, 'Oh! Just what I wanted.' As there was only room for one, and they wanted to be together they made me get in. The occupants were a family from Lancashire, who were on their way to Bournemouth for a holiday. Luckily it is quite easy to get a lift near where the Ringwood Road joins the main London Bournemouth one. Within a few moments of being put down I signalled a huge Rolls-Royce. It really was a lovely car and I thoroughly enjoyed my comfortable ride at a pretty good speed to Lyndhurst. This car was in actual fact a taxi. The driver told me he had taken some people from Southend to Bournemouth in the morning and now he was on his way back. How I wished; I was wanting a lift at least home if not all the way to London. When I got to Lyndhurst I knew that I only had about half an hour in which to get the boat. I began walking out of Lyndhurst when a private car stopped and I got to Lymington with a very charming woman and her two nieces. They left me at the turning to Bournemouth and I rushed down to the station to find that I had made it. I had about five minutes to wait for the train to take me down to the ferry. I really was most relieved and it was certainly a lovely peaceful rest I found on the way across.

IX

Bridgwater to Willersey

On the second Saturday in September I arranged to go up to Willersey to stay with John and Kay. John was home on leave but was returning at the beginning of the next week. I forget how I got to Bridgwater to Weston Zoyland but I presume that I got a lift. Anyway I was not long in Bridgwater before I got a lift in the front seat of a lorry. I was surprised when we took the Weston-Super-Mare turning but I was informed that a lot of heavy lorries go that way to avoid the climb up the Mendips We stopped for a drink at a pub just the other side the Weston and then on to Bristol. He left me at the southern end of the city but I managed to get a private car a little way down the bypass and then several of us got into a big army lorry and we were put down a mile or so from Filton. There two of us were lucky in getting a small private car out onto the main road again and a little way along towards Gloucester. The worst thing about hitching, I always find, is getting landed on the wrong side of a large town or city, especially when I do not know it very well. By now I know the ins and outs of several of the most important ones, including Bristol, Salisbury and Reading. After a little time I got a lift in a private car with a middle-aged man. I was lucky really as, when we passed the roundabout at Filton, there were a great many service people waiting for lifts. I was amazed to see so many of them standing at the roundabout instead of going a little way along the road. There are not many drivers who will stop there especially on a busy road. Soon after we started the driver said 'I'm nearly out of petrol. Let me know when you see a garage.'

'All right,' I said 'I hope you come to one soon'. This was still during the time when all the garages were not open and quite often they had no petrol anyway. The situation improved immensely in the following few months. We passed one garage but as there was one car being filled and another waiting we decided to go on to the next one. Suddenly there was that horribly disquieting noise that tells the tale of an empty tank and then the peace and quiet descended as we cruised down a small slope and came to a stop at the side of the road. 'You stay here and I'll go on and see if there is a garage,' said the driver. I sat for about five minutes until he returned to say the owner of the garage was at a café a few hundred yards back. I decided to accompany him to the café as I hate sitting still not knowing what is happening. Not far down the road, was 'The Orange Umbrella'. It was just a hut, but as it was in the midst of being painted with orange windowsills by a lad of about sixteen it looked as if it might be quite nice. Anyway we went in and found the owner of both garage and café was out with his wife for the afternoon. The next most obvious thing to do was eat. Salad and eggs were not only asked for but produced by a small girl. It was a good meal, especially when supplemented by another helping of salad and bread-and-butter. After tea I had the idea of asking the boy who was outside painting if he had a bicycle as the next garage was a mile away. He had a bicycle but came back with the sad news that there was no petrol there. Then I suggested that we asked the owners of any of the cars parked outside the cafe if they had any petrol in cans. As one party came out we told them of our plight and they said they had some. Having filled up and given coupons we were once more on our way. The man I was with was only going to Stroud, but he was so worried that I would not get in before dark that he insisted on taking me all the way to Cheltenham. We picked up another WAAF at Gloucester and I got off in the High Street in Cheltenham. The WAAF wanted to go up towards Leckhampton so got a lift all the way as that is the way out of Cheltenham to Stroud. I was really most grateful for this kindness as I could quite easily have got a lift when he ran out of petrol but one doesn't like to leave anyone when they're in a fix like that. I walked to Pittville Park gates and there got a lift to Winchcombe. It was then not very long before a private car came along. He was going to Chipping Camden but went via Willersey for me. The distance either way is about the same so that was all right. I got to Willersey before it was dark and was very glad to be able to sink into a chair and have a nice rest.

X

Broadway to Bridgwater

I had to return to Weston Zoyland on Sunday, September
9 So John and Kay took me by car into Broadway to make
it easier for me. It had been a short but pleasant visit and
there was no doubt that my pass finished at midnight on
Sunday. It was just after three o'clock when I was left in
Broadway and in about five minutes I got a lift with a man
and his wife in a private car. When I got in they asked if I
could map read. Said I could so they gave me a big map
and asked which way anyone going from Axminster to
Birmingham would go. I told them up as far as
Tewkesbury, so we branched off to that lovely old town
and turned off to Gloucester. They were trying to intercept
their son, who was doing the journey to Birmingham.
They left me just outside Gloucester in case they missed
him coming through the town. Almost at once I got a lift
with a dignitary of the church into Gloucester and walked
to the main Bristol road. I had not long to wait before I
got a lift in a private car with a man who was going to
Bristol. He was on his way back from leave in Wales. It
was a pleasant run and he dropped me on the North side

of Bristol. I was very lucky as I was making for the bus stop as I stopped a car with two men in it who took me almost to the top of Bedminster, the Bridgwater side of Bristol. As I got to the top a very nice Australian stopped and gave me a lift a few miles. There was a lot of traffic on the road but the cars all seemed to be full up but eventually I got a lift in a private car to Churchill, where the Stroud, Weston-Super-Mare main road crossed the A38. Then I was very lucky as I got into a car with a dear old couple who had been up to see their son whose ship was in dock there. They were, I think going down to Plymouth but maybe not so far. Anyway they dropped me at Bridgwater and I was able to get a bus out to Weston Zoyland.

XI

Bridgwater to Hook

Just after twelve o'clock on the 22 of September, a Saturday I set off with three lifts to Taunton, or rather to the turning about half a mile out of the town. Then I got a lift in a lorry a few miles and I should really have gone on that way but the driver told me to go down another road to get to Salisbury and after getting a car a few miles I got another back to the Yeovil road again. I then had a ride in a rather rickety car with a farmer and his small son and daughter for about four miles. It was after this that my luck changed and I got a ride in a lorry all the way down to Yeovil, which is, of course on the main London road. Here I got a lift in a big taxi to Sherborne and almost at once I got a lift with a very nice young couple who had come all the way from Tintagel and were, joy of joys, going up to London. We reached Hook at half past five and I was very glad to be home if only for one night.

XII

Weston Zoyland to Winchfield

On Saturday, December 1, I set off quite early and got down to Taunton. It was a cold day but fortunately not wet. I had some time to wait at Taunton as the traffic at that hour of the morning was very slight. At last a small utility came along with an army officer being driven to Salisbury. That suited me fine and I was very pleased with life as we sped along. I made a mistake in Salisbury not knowing the roads. I asked someone and they told me the wrong one and I get a lorry much too far north where I met some men hitching who said there was no traffic on the road but I soon stopped a car and the owner took me almost to Basingstoke. Then I got a lift to the garage at the top of Basingstoke and another to the Dorchester Arms near Hook. Here an R.A.C. man in a little car not only took me to Hartley Wintney but helped me to find Winchfield and the Rectory where I was going for the first time. This was certainly a stroke of luck as I now know having walked the 2 miles several times. The next day I returned to the camp by train so as to arrive back as late as possible.

XIII

Various Half-Forgotten Journeys

Usually after hitching I make notes if I have not time to record my journey at once in this book but occasionally I have even forgotten to do that and as time went on I did more journeys and got behind with writing some of my travels which have been left out, but in this chapter I am going to comment on what I can remember of some of them though I'm writing over a year later than most of them.

After frantic notes and calculations for a year when I kept no diary I have found five journeys which have been left out of this book. Three of these were to Cheltenham on November 3 and 24, and December 8 of 1945. All from Weston Zoyland and in each case I hitched back as well. Details I cannot remember but of the first, one incident stands out clearly. I was with my friend from Chile, Cherry Duncan and we had decided to up to Cheltenham to see Anne Horsfall and Margery [Bremridge, who in 1962 would let us stay in her Surrey home on our return from New Zealand with our three sons], who were still there. [Cheltenham Ladies College]

After various lifts we got on a furniture van at Bristol, which took us most of the way but before we got to Gloucester a tyre burst with a resounding bang which woke Cherry up with a start from her sleep with her head on my shoulder. How we got back the following day I forget but we both enjoyed it while it lasted.

Then, on the 24th I had nothing to do on camp so set off to Cheltenham one more. I had a car to … [There is a blank here] a few miles from Bridgwater and the driver very kindly signalled a passing American lorry which not only stopped but took me at breakneck speed to Cheltenham. He was destined for Prestwick, Scotland but knowing some people in Cheltenham he took me there and decided to stay the night and I was there in time to watch the 1st XI hockey match at half past two, having left camp at twelve o'clock or it may even have been half past by the time I had changed and got ready. Once again I can remember that I hitched back on the Sunday, but exactly how I have no idea at all. Two weekends later I hitched to Cheltenham once more to be in a match against the College and I was to meet Bunny at the station. [This would have been Sheila – Bunny Miller, one of my best friends at College who had also been asked to play for the Old Girls] I don't remember how I got to Gloucester but it was getting dark by then and I got a car about halfway, then I was very lucky and got a lift in a big car right down the Prom so I was able to pop up to the hostel with my things and then I just got to the station before Bunny's train got in.

The next day I was to play hockey for Weston Zoyland so I caught an early train to Bristol and was lucky in getting a car straight down to Bridgwater. Arriving on camp I found the match had been scratched so I need not have hurried nearly so much. I have not been to Cheltenham since then, as I as I now have no particular friends there to go and see.

Previous to these journeys, on October 13 I was really fed up that weekend. I set off for the Isle of Wight. I remember but little of the journey except a kind couple who are going to Weymouth and dropped me at Dorchester and there a dear lady took me to Bournemouth. When talking about hitching she came out with the prize remark, 'Of course you never take lifts with men do you?' I was torn between politeness not to offend her and the need to be truthful, so I had to explain very tactfully that there were very few women drivers now-a-days and really all the men who had given me lifts had been very decent. She said her husband would never give lifts to girls by themselves if he were alone. I wondered.

I had to get a bus in Bournemouth and another to Southampton as it was getting dark and anyway the last boat had gone. I was thoroughly miserable by then and was rather dismayed when the hostel I usually go to was full but they took me in when I said I was all alone and there seemed to be an awful lot of Americans around the town! The next morning I was up bright and early and got a lift somehow right up to Hook where I breezed in on Mummie, who was just starting life in her caravan in the drive. The new tenants had just arrived and I was introduced to Mrs Fradgely. Mummie was most surprised to see me and invited me to stay for lunch, which I did and I set off once more about two o'clock. The last

Mummie saw of me was climbing into the back of an open sports car already occupied by four men, one of which was almost on the floor and comfortably (or otherwise) wrapped up in a blanket to keep warm. [Shades of things to come in 1950 when a similar car with 4 young men stopped, asking Richard and me if we would like a lift as we toiled with our heavily laden bicycles up La Spezia mountain on our way from Rome to Marseilles. In fact they took 2 leather straps from their luggage and the men in the back held them out for us to hold and we were pulled precariously to the top. This was September 17, our first wedding anniversary. We celebrated it in an eating chestnut grove.]

Just beyond Andover was their destination and we tore along at great speed. About a mile away from where they were making they ran out of petrol. Two of them went off and I stopped a car for a lift. Of course it had to be occupied by a WAAF Wing Officer who told me to put on my hat, luckily they were not 'Going my way'. The next car I stopped was a real stroke of luck. It was a small car with a couple in it who were, I think going to Birmingham, or perhaps not quite so far. Anyway hey took me on the lovely run up to Marlborough and I was very tempted to go on to Cheltenham but I resisted that and later rather regretted it. Somehow one of my next lifts took me down the Devizes way and it was at Trowbridge that I finally got stuck. It was getting dark and I had a long wait for a train to Bath so tried to hitch but none of the cars would stop and having missed the last Bridgwater train at Bath I had to stay in Bristol. I met a very nice woman on the train and she insisted on my going home

50

with them and her small daughter, who was sitting on my knee. They were most kind to me and in the morning I was up early to get the first train down which just got back on camp in time.

When Christmas 1945 came we could only have a pass if we could get home without using the trains. I was going down to Beer and decided to hitch. I set off early in the morning of the 22nd which was once again on Saturday. Somehow I got to North Petherton just south of Taunton and then I got another lift to Taunton where there was a very thick mist. I was in a farm lorry and sitting on a farmer's knee. My leg went to sleep and I had difficulty in standing when I got out. The mist being thick the traffic was slow so when a lorry went slowly by I was easily able to stop it and I was whisked off to Illminster. The mist was only local and we were very soon clear of it. I had some time to wait before I got a lift with two men in a car, to Chard. From there I got a lift to Axminster, stopping on the way to put down a small daughter of the woman driving the car, to go out riding with a groom. They talked enthusiastically of the turkey they had and the Goose which Grandma had brought when inviting herself for Christmas. Anyway we did well ourselves with duck. From Axminster onwards was slow and I had a long wait before leaving Ax. This lift only took me a few miles and the next turned off to Exeter and I was tempted to go that way and walk down into Beer from the top road. I was glad that I did not. There was an A.A. man at the crossroads and he stopped the next car and asked the occupants to take me to Seaton, which they very kindly did, arriving just in time for a bus to Beer. This was a long journey and I have since done the return one in much less time.

Pages 61 to 87 are blank except for Chapter XIV heading. It restarts with Chapter XVII. But I have two scraps of paper with notes on including Chapter XV

XIV

Winchfield to Isle of Wight and Back

Friday, January 11.

1 One man at the end of Winchfield Road to the main road.

2 Man with new family to Hook.

3 With sailor to Salisbury turning. (Sat in the back.)

4 With sailor to Chandler's Ford. Big car and fast. Conservative. (houses finished) Sat in front, to Chandler's Ford. With sailor to Portsmouth.

5 Ex-RAF to the bridge at Southampton.

6 Car to 2 1/2 miles from Lymington.

7 Traveller's van to Lymington.

8 Taxi lift from Yarmouth to Cotswold. [This was Ron and Nan Drake's home at the bottom of The Avenue in Freshwater, near the Memorial Hall, where I was billeted when on the Radar Station. We used to play table tennis in the Memorial Hall. The foundation stone laid by Hallam, Lord Tennyson]

Saturday, January 12. With Bombshells ENSA bods. [ENSA. The Entertainments National Service Association. Set up in 1939 by Basil Dean and Leslie Henson to provide entertainment for the troops. During the whole war they suffered only one casualty] F/O to Hartley Whitney. [Not sure how I got to Winchfield from here.]

XV

Weston Zoyland to Winchfield

February 1 Weston Zoyland to Winchfield with friend Jill. Left eleven o'clock.

1 Transport to Bridgwater.

2 Open small truck to near Bristol.

3 Woman in car to bridge near Bristol.

4 Hailstorm in Bath Road, Rudloe Manor.[Not knowing that in 1947 I would be stationed there and go on the back of a motorbike to Ascot with my friend Humphrey Wakefield for my 21st birthday. Uncle Edwin was there and we celebrated in the Royal Hotel. My mother and I had our caravans in Englemere Farm]. Cramped in lorry.

5 Car to Chippenham with mother and son.

6 Car to Calne.

7 Stuffy RAF transport to Reading. Left Jill and two others. Cpl and self to Blackbush. [Not knowing that in 1949, my new sister-in-law Pam Hutchings would start

flying from there as an air hostess and would meet her husband to be, Ron Codrai. Also that we would meet twice in Nice airport, both while cycling to and back from Rome in 1950. On each occasion her plane arrived just as we did].

8 Lorry to Hartley Whitney with... to Winchfield station. From there I walked to the Rectory where I had my caravan, arriving at ten past one. [My mother had her caravan there as well since we had moved from Ascot.]

XVI

Weston Zoyland to Winchfield

No notes on this.

XVII

London to Luton and Back

On Saturday, February 9 I was staying at the YWCA in
Baker Street and was to be in Luton in time for Jill's
wedding at 12 o'clock. It was, I think, about nine when I
set out on a bus for Golders Green. There I waited 5
minutes and got a lift in an army lorry to Barnet. [Not
knowing that in 2000 I would spend the night in Barnet
hospital with a badly sprained leg having fallen in the
lorry park at Mimms Service Station. But that's another
story] I did not seem able to get a lift from there so I went
into a small newspaper shop at the bottom of the hill to
get some change for a bus. As I came out of big lorry
stopped and the driver said he was going to Manchester.
At St Albans he put me down in the centre of the town
and I walked through onto the Luton Road. It was rather
difficult getting through. That was obviously market day.
I saw lots of lemons at one stall but also a very long
queue. After a wait of about 10 minutes I got a lift in a
private car, the front seat of which was full of hats. From
St Albans to Luton I had lovely music to listen to. I also
learned that Luton's main industry and reason for its

existence is the millinery trade. I got a shock when I saw Luton it was such a different view from the one looking at St Albans. The houses all seemed huddled together and it all looked dismal and dirty. I would never want to live there but I like St Albans very much and all the surrounding country. It reminded me of Hampshire. After a very nice wedding I began to wend my way back home. At half past three I left Luton and was just making for Castle Hill where I was more likely to get a lift when I saw a lorry coming up the road. 'No harm in trying' I thought holding up my hand and the driver stopped. He said he was going to St Albans and then it turned out that he was going all the way to London. We got to Waterloo at 4.50 so I decided to catch the 4.54 train to Winchfield instead of going down to Staines to get a lift with darkness coming about a quarter to six.

XVIII

Chivenor to Porlock and Back

On Sunday, February 17 I was spending my first weekend at Chivenor aerodrome. I had nothing special to do so I decided that unless it was a sunny day I would stay in and be really lazy. As it turned out it was a lovely bright morning so I got up at nine o'clock and by quarter to ten I was walking out of the 'drome with a very carefree feeling and nowhere in particular to go.

The sun was really quite warm so I didn't mind walking and I soon got a lift with a man into Barnstable. On the way we picked up an airman. We were in Barnstaple in a few minutes for although the car was small we did a steady 50 to 60 miles an hour all the way. When I got to Barnstable I was undecided as to which way to go. I had the choice of three ways, the Bideford Road, the Lynton Road or the Exeter to Taunton one. Just as I had begun walking along the latter road a car came along but did not stop until he had gone about fifty yards. When I got in I said, 'Are you going towards Exeter?'

'No,' said the driver. 'We are going to South Molton.'

'I don't know where that is but I'll come,' I said. They were most surprised that I didn't mind where I went, until I explained. It was a very pretty run and the sun was still shining when they put me down about four miles from South Molton. I began walking but soon got a lift to South Moulton. I walked through the town and down a hill. A few cars passed me and then one with three men, the driver being an Army Sergeant, stopped. I got in and they said they were going to Dulverton which was a few miles north of Bampton on the way to Minehead. It was at this point that I decided what I would like to do. If I could get to Minehead I reckoned on being able to get back to Barnstable along the coast. We did not go right into Bampton but took a short cut down a long, winding narrow road as they were going to Dulverton station. They left me to walk the few hundred yards over a quaint little bridge spanning the R. Exe, back into Devon, for I was by then in Somerset, having crossed the border just after leaving the main road. It was by now about a quarter to twelve and it was not until about half past one that I got another lift. In the usual way that would certainly have dampened my spirits a bit but I was in no hurry and the sun and the scenery were so lovely that I thoroughly enjoyed the walk. I did not go very far at first but sat on a big log at the confluence of the River Exe and its tributary the R. Barle. I did not know then what river it was so I got out my map and traced it right the way up to Exmoor where it begins (a few miles from Simon's Bath on the Exe Plain 55 miles from the sea at Exmouth) I went on walking and crossed once more into Somerset. After about 3 miles I took off my battledress top as I was so warm. Just as I had done this I heard a car coming, but I

61

was quite prepared for it to go past as quite a few had already done so. Anyway it stopped and I jumped in the back. They were going to Porlock! When I looked at the map I discovered that Porlock was on the coast, and nearer Barnstable than Minehead. My life had certainly changed. The occupants of the car were a woman driving with her mother in the back with me and her grandmother, aged 82 in the front. They told me that it was a post war car. It was certainly very comfortable and seemed to run well. Just before coming to Nutcombe at the inn called the 'Rest and be Thankful' we turned off to the left. We had got nearly as far as Exford before we realised we had missed a turning about four miles back. We turned round and were soon going uphill along a road with high beech hedges either side. I was surprised at the number of beech hedges there were round this part. The beauty of them being that they still had their autumn coloured leaves on.

We then came to the end of the hedges but I had to get out and open a gate for us to go through. From this point until I got back I went through some of the most lovely country I have ever seen. We passed very near the top of Dunkery Beacon from where, on a clear day seven counties can be seen. These include the Welsh ones just across the Bristol Channel. Unfortunately it was rather hazy, but even so the view was good. Coming down very steep hills into Porlock we could just make out the sea in the little coves and bays below. It must be simply glorious up there when the heather and gorse are out. At Porlock I went too far down towards the sea, but got a lift back to the Lynmouth turning, which I had not seen on the way through in the other car. There was an A.A. man at the

junction of the main road and the toll road. I asked him
what the traffic was like and he said it should not be long
before I got a lift. There was no point in walking on as
there were two different routes and both went straight up
hill from the village. A man came along and asked the
A.A. Scout the way to some farm and then said 'Where do
you want to go? 'Lynmouth please 'I said. But
unfortunately he was going to Minehead but he said he
was going to Barnstable the next day, which did not help
much. Very soon a big car drew up and I was comfortably
settled in the back with the driver and two girls in the
front. We took the main road and it was amazing how
steeply it went up. The view was not much but most of the
way we got occasional glimpses of the sea to the North
and Exmoor stretched out bleak but majestic to the South.
Coming down Countisbury Hill into Lynmouth was a very
slow process for though it looks very easy it is in actual
fact one of the most dangerous hills in the area. The side
of the hill goes straight up to the left and straight down to
the sea to the right. The danger lies in the nasty corners on
the way. On the opposite side of the bay and directly in
front of us as we descended was the little town of Lynton,
perched precariously on the side of the cliff. The houses,
especially the hotels looked really enormous and likely to
fall off at the slightest puff of wind. It was cold as I stood
at the corner of the street in Lynmouth, which at first sight
looked like a little Swiss village. Being on the north coast
meant that the sun had already set behind the huge hills
behind the town. [On August 15/16 1952 when our son
Keith was 7 months old, in New Zealand, the disastrous
flood engulfed Lynmouth. There are dramatic images and
the full story on line. Years later we will discover the

large funicular Lynton and Lynmouth Cliff Railway linking the two towns. It is powered only by water coming from the River Lyn. It was opened on Easter Sunday 1890, also all on line.] A peculiarity about the place is that to get to Lynton there are two roads. One goes straight up for half a mile and there you are in Lynton. By the other route you go in and out of the hills for five and a half miles before you reach the town. As I stood waiting and hoping I was also wondering by which road I would eventually get up. Presently a young couple came up and the man asked, 'Do you know if there is anywhere round here that we could get a cup of tea?'

'I'm afraid I don't know this place, at all,' I said, 'but I should imagine Lynton would be better, this place looks a bit dead!'

'I'll go back and get the car, you wait here,' said the man. As he went I turned to the girl and we chatted for a bit and it turned out that they were staying in Barnstable and were returning there after having a much-needed cup of tea. She invited me to join them so when her husband came back we both got in and I said, 'Are we going half a mile up or five and a half round?'

'Oh! Straight up, of course, 'said the husband and up we went. We went into a very nice hotel there and had to wait until four o'clock, twenty minutes for tea. As we were standing round a huge log fire the man said, 'we must introduce ourselves, I'm Ian – Yvonne,' pointing to his wife. 'Elizabeth' said I and that was that. We had a pleasant tea and left Lynton just before five o'clock. I was in the back and with my own half inch map and their 1 inch Ordnance Survey map I did the guiding home. They

64

insisted on taking me all the way to Chivenor and so we decided to cut across country and approach Barnstable from the North and Chivenor. This plan fell through as the sun was low and rather strong for Ian, who was driving, so at Kentisbury Ford we continued on the main road by taking a sharp turn to the left. Actually it was at Blackmoor Gate that we decided to make straight for Barnstable. It was there that my half inch colour map came in useful for at a glance it could be seen that the main road was not nearly so hilly as the more pleasing looking one to the left by Bratton Fleming. From here onwards the country is no longer awe-inspiring but exceedingly pretty, rather like South Devon in many ways. By now, of course, we were back in Devon having crossed the border at County Gate between Porlock and Lynton. Ian and Yvonne were very kind and took me right back to camp where I arrived at twenty to six after a very happy day. 81 miles.

XIX

Chivenor to Westward Ho! And Back

On the day after my visit and all round by Porlock I had to work in the morning and evening so I decided to pop down to Westward Ho! in the afternoon. I left camp just before two o'clock and within a few minutes got a lift into Barnstable in a private car. I was walking over the bridge towards Bideford when a small van and I was taken up to the top of the hill, which is easier for hitching, as the road is wider and more deserted. A private car whizzed past and so did a lorry with Bideford written on the door. Then along came a small car with two men in the front. They were going all the way to Bideford, which suited me fine. By this time I had not definitely decided to go to Westward Ho! but they told me it was easy to get there and well worth seeing. They also said I should go to Appledore, which is on the opposite side of the River Torridge from Instow. They said it was a very quaint little place, but unfortunately I never went down there that day. I crossed the bridge at Bideford and walked a little way through the town and then I got a lift to Northam, and was told it was not very far to Westward Ho! Unfortunately the weather was very bad although it was not raining hard there was a steady drizzle. I began walking and soon got a lift. The driver told me that when he bought his house it was the only one there. Now the place has a lot of houses and quite a few shops and hotels.

On a really sunny day I would have liked it much better. There are some lovely sands there and I should think the walks in the surrounding countryside would be some of the most enjoyable. I walked some way along the sands by the Pebble Ridge, the like of which I have never seen before. I would not have thought it was possible. For about three miles there is a ridge of big grey stones washed up by the tides of many years. Having bought a couple of pounds of oranges it was not long before an airman on leave, with his mother took me back to Northam. I would have liked to go down to Appledore but decided I did not want to risk being back late so I decided against it. I got a lift in a van back to Bideford and the offer of a lift to Clovelly on the following Wednesday if I was in Bideford by two thirty but I did not think it was likely I would turn up.

I walked back across the bridge and at the top of a small hill I got a ride in a jeep with a REME Lieutenant and his driver. They only took me to Instone but there I got a lift in a big taxi. During the course of our conversation I discovered that he had a garage in Mortehoe. Luckily I knew that that was the other side of Chivenor on the coast near *Woolacombe, so I asked him to drop me at Chivenor instead of leaving me in Barnstable. I had certainly enjoyed my outing but I would have liked some sunshine. I decided if I stayed long enough I would return there and see Appledore and Westward Ho! bathed in sunshine. 34 miles

*It would be on September 7, 1991 that Richard and I would spend the afternoon overlooking Woolacombe Bay. This was Richard's last glimpse of the sea, for he died shortly after our return to Wordsworth's home, Alfoxton near Holford after a wonderful last day together. We scattered his ashes near the Tennyson Monument on September the 17th, our 42nd wedding anniversary and his seat is there. RICHARD J HUTCHINGS AUTHOR AND PRESIDENT OF THE FARRINGFORD TENNYSON SOCIETY.

XX

Chivenor to Clovelly and Back

On the day before I returned to Weston Zoyland from Wrafton I decided to go down to Clovelly, as it was such a glorious afternoon. That was on Wednesday, February 27. I asked one of the airmen at Wrafton with me and we went as far as Bideford on the football team transport. We had to walk up a few steep hills in Bideford before we reached level ground on the main road. A car passed us but stopped only a few yards further on. As we were walking along the same car passed again. But this time the driver said he had not stopped the first time as he had as he had a call to make a call and didn't know how long he might be. He took us all the way to the turning off to the right to Clovelly, about 2 miles away. He was going to Hartland and said he would be returning between half past four and a quarter to five. So we said we would probably be on the road again by then but he was not to wait for us if we were not there. It is quite a long walk down to Clovelly but it is certainly worth it. The woods just before the village were lovely but in summer they must be really glorious, especially with the blue sea as the background with Lundy Island rising out of its midst.

Clovelly itself just consists of one very narrow, steep, cobbled road or path where no traffic can go at all. The houses are old and quaint. We did not walk down the hill as we wanted to get back, but someday I shall return, when I have more time to explore right down to the quay. We did not even see any of the donkeys which are used to carry people but we saw sledges with sacks of coal outside a few of the cottages.

We hurried back and waited on the main road for about ten minutes. Then a car came along and we got in, as we did not want to wait for the other car in case he had already gone. We learned later that he had come along a bit later on and gone right down nearly to the quay to look for us. As it turned out we did very well as the car into which we got was going to Ilfracombe so we asked them to put us down at Barnstable where we had a very good meal and went to the cinema.

XXI

Bridgwater to Beer

Notes on scrap of paper.

Feb. 28, 1946. Dep. 12.00. 4 hours 10 minutes.

1 Private car to Taunton with man and wife.

2 R.N. Plymouth lorry. To Exeter right A3085.
(Transport café)

3 Exeter bypass A35 halfway Hotel America.

4 Man in car to Sidmouth.

5 Man and two children to Sidford.

6 Big yellow car to top of hill.

7 Man and wife to Bovey lane. Arr. Beer 16.10

XXII

Beer to Plymouth and Back

Saturday March 2.

1 9.15. Car to Sidford. AA or RAC Inspector of pubs.
2 Lady to Plymouth and back.

[Just a tiny scrap of paper. A pity nothing else]

XXIII

Beer to Bridgwater

Sunday March 3.

    1 2 men 1 woman to Sidford

    2 To Ottery turning. (Bowd)

    3 To Newton Poppleford. Man and woman and Army officer. ([going to] Budleigh)

    4 Man and wife to Exeter (A38)

    5 Boy and girl to Pinhay.

    6 5 miles from Cullompton man and wife with little girl.

    7 Man and 2 women to **Wellington** Cross.

    8 Ambulance via Taunton to collect????? to Bridgwater. [Thence to camp at Weston Zoyland] [Scrap of paper]

XXIV

Weston Zoyland to Porlock and Back

On Sunday March 10 Kay and I got up for breakfast, an
unusual procedure for Sunday especially as I had been to
a dance the night before. After making marmalade and
spam sandwiches and having been given a bar of
chocolate by Ruth we set off at ten to ten. We had
Minehead in mind as our objective but really, we did not
mind where we ended up. It was Kay's first experience of
hitching. It was a lovely sunny day so we set off at quite a
brisk pace towards Bridgwater. It was not long before we
were given a lift in an N.F.S. van. Just after that we
picked up another WAAF from Weston Zoyland who was
only going to the village. As we were walking towards the
Minehead road, up past the 'Odeon' I signalled a car
which stopped. They were going to Bishop's Lydiard ten
miles from Williton, but south of it. We went right up
over the Quantocks passing first through Enmore. The
scenery was lovely, the snow, which was still lying in
these parts being very effective. We were taken just
through Bishop's Lydeard to the main road to Williton.

Just as we began walking along a deserted road Kay discovered that she had left her hat in the car, but it was too late to do anything about it, except that they had told us their name, and also that they knew the owners of the farm on our camp. The one joy was that we still had our sandwiches with us.

We decided to walk on rather than stand about waiting for a lift. After just over a mile a small, rather ramshackle car came along with a man and girl in it. They had a big Ordinance Survey map with them. They took us to St Audries and were truly surprised when we said we really did not know where we were going eventually. Then once more we began walking, but this time with greater confidence as we were on the main Taunton to Minehead road. That is the A39 road along which I travelled during my stay at Chivenor, when I visited Clovelly and also when I was hitching from Porlock to Barnstable. One of these days I shall probably be coming across it in Cornwall beyond Bude and Camelford. As we tramped on we began to feel hungry, especially as we had been walking for some distance and still no car would pick us up. Even a small army transport passed us and the occupants only waved. It made us mad to see them do that but we kept our spirits up. 'We won't have lunch until we get out of our next lift,' I said, and Kay agreed though as we neared Williton were both looking for a convenient gate on which to sit and eat those welcome sandwiches. [As I was dictating this in 2015 Simon came in and I reminded him that it was at Williton that we bought a huge turkey breast on Christmas Eve in 1992. We were on our way to spend Christmas up near Dunkery Beacon.

There was enough left for us to take on to Bath, where we stayed with Corrine Wimpress, daughter of Richard's first publisher Mr Sandie of Brodies.]

Then, just as we crossed the railway bridge before the town I saw a car racing along. I urged Kay to run and we got over the bridge so they would see our signal more easily and not have to stop too suddenly. They stopped and in we jumped, disturbing, I'm sorry to say a young girl who was dozing in the back. They took us all the way to Minehead, where we arrived at about ten to one. Then we hurried through the town, which struck both of us as being very nice indeed, the streets being broad and not too many shops to clutter up the place. We caught glimpses of the sea but did not go down to the front. We walked out towards Porlock and decided to eat when we had left all houses behind. 'Let's just get round this corner,' I said as the last of the houses was in sight. Having agreed on this we were delighted to find first a bench and then a seat in a sheltered spot on the corner. Those sandwiches certainly tasted good. The only thing we then lacked was a drink and we did not like to go into anyone's house at lunchtime so we contented ourselves with the hope that if we got to Porlock we could get some there.

We walked up the hill to where the other part of the main road joins the part that goes through the town. There we just got sat on a gate when a car came along. It was a man and his daughter, who, we gathered was in the WAAF. At one time, she used to hitch to Minehead from Bath in about three and a half hours. They took us to the turning down to Luccombe. Once more our walking began. Two boys passed us on bicycles and called asking if we wanted a lift. 'No, we'd rather have this car, thanks,' I said as one came in sight. It would have been good if only it had stopped but of course it did not. The boys were soon out of sight and another car came and they gave us a lift to Porlock. The driver was a dear old man, and he had his wife with him. She had not been out for months, having had double pneumonia and pleurisy. [The same as me in Christchurch, New Zealand in 1960.] They took us round some quaint little roads in Porlock and then left us to make their way back to Minehead.

Having found a place to do our hair and freshen up generally we took a look around Porlock. When I passed through before I had not had time for loitering as I was some way from my destination – Barnstable. We walked up to the bottom of Porlock Hill and there met the same A.A. Scout who had been there the first time. He recognised me and asked how I got on so I told him my good luck on that particular Sunday. Then we went into the quaint little 'Ship Inn' where I would like to stay sometime – in fact Kay and I want to do that some weekend and then take a real look at some of the Doone country. It was after hours but as we only wanted water to quench our thirst they were able to give us that.

As we walked back I saw in A shop window a whole row of cloth-bound Bartholomew's map, things I have tried everywhere to get, and also some nice editions of Lorna Doone, which I had had difficulty in getting in Sidmouth a week or so previously. Unfortunately, being Sunday, I was unable to get them. We walked up a hill a little way out of Porlock. We thought we heard a car coming as we neared the top of the hill so Kay made me run to the top, where we stood gasping for breath but no car came along. We rewarded ourselves with a couple of pieces of Ruth's chocolate cake each. Then we passed a stationary car and hurried by in case it should move without the driver seeing us. Several cars then passed us by but the original one stopped. We did not go straight to Minehead as the man had some business at a little cottage down to the right off the main road. We lay back in this very comfortable car and could quite easily have slept. At Minehead Kay saw a little boy with what she thought was a choc ice. We hurried down to the front and into a little café where they gave us each a fourpenny choc ice. We sat and ate them with gusto. They really were excellent. Kay nearly left her bag behind but after a gentle hint from me turned round and took it off the back of the chair. As we walked out of Minehead we got a lift with a very nice ex ATS girl who had been to visit a friend in hospital in Minehead and was now on the way back to Williton. She had been stationed at Hendon on heavy Ack. After this the fun began! We walked through Williton, missing the bus by five seconds on purpose of course as buses always make me feel not as good as I might if you see what I mean. We crossed the railway bridge once more and decided we were hungry. It was really terribly amusing, as each time a car came along we stuffed the sandwiches back in the bag. We must have looked a really scruffy sight strolling along, hatless and grubby munching away with a very carefree air at our spam sandwiches. We were nearly in hysterics and just as I, out of defiance because no car would stop for us, had put in an extra big mouthful a lovely big car came along. We signalled it but I was too weak with laughing to do much about it. Fortunately it did not stop, as I'm sure we would have disgraced ourselves. Then at last a car stopped. The woman in front got out and took out the four or five-month-old baby boy, who was contentedly lying in a carrycot in the back. They had intended having him in front for a while so we were not making a nuisance of ourselves. Most of the way back to Bridgwater, for that was where they were going. Kay slept, peacefully – I thanked goodness that she doesn't snore! We returned through St Audries and Kilve, the latter being a very attractive village. [It would be in the room named Kilve that Richard would die in 1991] At Bridgwater we had crumpets, and the remains of our sandwiches and Kay had some tea and coffee for which I knew she had been dying. It was not long before we got a lift on the Weston Zoyland road with a couple were going through to Langport. We got back to the W.A.A.F. site at ten past six both feeling tired but happy.

XXV

Weston Zoyland to Winchfield and Back

On Saturday March 23, the accountant officer at Weston Zoyland was motoring down to Southampton, leaving camp at half past eleven. Having arranged to go home that weekend this lift was most useful. He had another WAAF in the back, whom he was taking all the way to Southampton. I intended going on Saturday and returning on Monday but it turned out differently as will be seen later on. We could not have chosen a better day for motoring. The sun was really warm and it made the journey very pleasant. The others left me in Salisbury and I walked a little way along the A30 road. I had a wait of about quarter of an hour for which I was rewarded with a lift all the way to Hartley Wintney. It was in a fairly big private car with a couple who were going from Bridport to London. They had some precious eggs.

I had walked just beyond Winchfield station and was not expecting a lift when a private car overtook me and then stopped and waited until I caught up. The driver said he could only take me a little way along the road as I got in. I told him that I was only going to the Rectory and he said he was too so I got taken right to the door. This was certainly a most fortunate lift as I met him at a party that evening as he offered to take me back to Salisbury the next day. I had not intended returning until Monday but on Sunday after church I decided to return and then get a long weekend later in the summer. My mother took me in the car to the Wellington Monument on the Reading – Basingstoke road and there we met Jack who is a cousin of the Barkers at the Rectory. [It would be from here that I would get married by Canon Barker to Richard Hutchings on September 17 1949. In 1967 we would call our new home in Newchurch on the Isle of Wight Winchfield Gardens. From here we would supply chrysanthemums for Princess Anne's twenty- first birthday at Buckingham Palace.] We had a lovely drive and I thoroughly enjoyed it. He took me to Wylie, which I at once recognised as the turning where Pam and I were dropped when I—

[Here unfortunately Book 1 of 2 ends abruptly though in pencil I have unaccountably written Stonehenge. In fact, at the back I have listed each chapter and this includes Chapter 26 Chivenor to Beer and Back but I fear that this appears to be missing. Chapter 1 in Book 2 shows I am still in Weston Zoyland, from where I was posted to Uxbridge just before taking up training to be an instructor for the EVT programme. Educational and Vocational Programme. My first posting being Blake Hall in Essex to teach dressmaking.]

Book II

I

Weston Zoyland to Plymouth and Back

Having got up early on Sunday morning, Ruth and I had breakfast and made lots of sandwiches, which we packed up with some oranges and chocolate. At ten to nine, on what promised to be as much of a scorcher as its predecessor, we set off from camp and walked along to the village of Weston Zoyland. We had no definite plans as to where we would go but we had Barnstable in mind. If possible we wanted to get to the coast somehow. Just as we got to the main road an open car passed us and stopped. The man was going to Bridgwater, which was a great blessing as Weston Zoyland is a very out of the way place, especially on a Sunday. We walked right through the town and a little way out on the Taunton road we got a lift in a small car with two men, who took us to North Petherton, a few miles from Bridgwater. They very kindly took us out of their way, just beyond the town. It was not long after that, about half past nine that a big car, with two men in front drew up in front of us. The passenger had a map so I had hopes of them going some distance. I was not disappointed. Having said they would take us to

Taunton, they said they were going to Plymouth. Our luck, we decided was definitely in. The day was lovely and the run down to Exeter and South Devon was really pleasant. It turned out that they were going to Newton Ferries, a few miles along the coast east of Plymouth. It looked very out of the way on the map so we tossed as to whether to go on or get off at Yealveton (pronounced YARTON). The answer was Plymouth but just as we were nearing Yealveton one of the men said. 'I'm sure you're going to change your minds.' I had an idea all the time that Ruth would like to go on, which she admitted so on we went. We arrived at Newton Ferries at half past eleven, or just after. The men were meeting a friend of theirs at one of the hotels there so they put us down just outside the hotel. Newton Ferries at once struck us as a most delightful spot. It reminded Ruth of 'Frenchman's Creek'. We saw a notice 'Boats for Hire' so immediately decided on a trip. Ruth had done no rowing but I was fairly confident having been on the river a lot at Stratford-upon-Avon. We had a small rowing boat and in spite of a wind I got it over to the Naas Mayo side of the river. There we sat on the beach and ate our sandwiches. We were very hungry. Then we collected a few shells as souvenirs and set off seawards to Yealm Mouth from where we would see Great Mewstone [From the old name for the herring gull. A large rocky island only half a mile off Wembury Point] in Wembury Bay. It got quite rough but Ruth wanted a shot at rowing so we took an oar each on the way back but I'm afraid I pulled a little harder so progress was slow. Then a little motorboat came alongside and the owner dropped a weight into our boat with a rope attached and we had a pleasant ride back.

Fortunately there were two post office telephone vans which took us to Brixton where they told us to walk northwards for a few miles to strike the A38 road again. I'm afraid Ruth came off worse which I had not realised at the time. She had the back of the van and I the front. She had a very uncomfortable journey and she could not see where she was going. The thought of walking in the heat of the day, it was now about half past one, rather appalled us so we began to eat two of our oranges. Then a car came along and in we got, for a ride all the way to Plymouth. It was very pleasant in Plymouth. We first of all went to the N.A.F.F.I club where we had a much-needed wash, in lovely hot water, and did our hair which was very blown about. By this time, I had dispensed with my battledress top and I'm afraid our hats had hardly been on our heads all day. We walked down to Plymouth Hoe, which was scattered with people lying on the grass, sunbathing. We did likewise for five minutes, but it being nearly three o'clock we decided to wend our way campward. It was some time before we got a lift out to Marsh Mills on the outskirts of the town. A Naval patrol had stopped for us but the driver said no traffic went that way and we'd better get a bus. A policeman told us which bus and where to get it and just then our lift turned up. The driver was a fair man. From Marsh Mills we refused the offer of a lift to Totnes as it is off the main road to Exeter but we might just as well have taken it as can be seen by subsequent events. We got a lift to Newton Abbot and were too comfortable to get out when we left the A38 road. In Newton Abbot we got a lift through Kingsteignton all the way to Teignmouth, where at five o'clock we had a quick coffee and orangeade and off we went again. We made a big mistake here by walking up the hill out of Teignmouth towards Dawlish. When we began it didn't seem as if it was very long but it was some time before we reached the top. Meanwhile many cars had passed without being able to stop. When we reached the top of a huge army staff car whizzed past but soon after a private car stopped of its own accord. An army captain was driving, with his father in front and his mother behind. We managed to squeeze in at the back. The driver had only been back from Burma a week. They took us all the way to Cullompton beyond Exeter having first visited a house, near to Exeter about buying a caravan. When they left us we got a lift in a private car with a man and woman and two small boys, who sat on the front seat together so that we could once more squeeze into the back. They took us to Waterloo Cross where the A373 from Tiverton joins the main road. Not long afterwards we got a lift to Wellington with a man and his wife. It was getting dark as we arrived in Wellington but if we caught the seven thirty bus we would miss the last one from Taunton at 8.5. Just as we were giving up in despair a small car stopped and when the driver had posted some letters he asked us if we wanted a lift. He was going to Hullavington so could get us to Taunton in time for our bus. We told this last driver of our adventures that day and his comment was, 'Aren't you scared of being caught in your working dress?'

'What do you know about working dress?' I said. 'Well I'm in the Air Force, too.' was his reply. It just shows that anyone nowadays might be in the services. I shall really give myself away in the wrong place one of these days.

To end the day we were back in Weston Zoyland by the quarter to nine bus feeling very weary but very glad we had had such a lovely time. 195 miles.

II

Weston Zoyland to West Looe and back via Launceston

On the weekend following our trip to Plymouth Ruth and I determined to get to Cornwall. We were off at twelve o'clock on Saturday, April 6 and by twenty to one we had packed up chocolate, sweets and biscuits to add to our haversack already filled with a few necessaries for the night. It was some time before we got a lift into Bridgwater and it especially peeved us when one of the officers from the camp passed us without stopping. Just before one we arrived in Bridgwater in a small private car with another WAAF to whom a lift was also being given. On the way we had passed one of the other girls, Elsie who was bicycling in. We went and bought some very nice sausage rolls and meat pasties. We also got a map of Cornwall to add to my collection and aid us if we ever reached that county. A private car came along just as we began walking to the main road. Along the road we saw Elsie so asked the driver to give her a lift as well, which he did. She was going to Exeter, where she lives. At North Petherton we nearly came to our doom as a huge removal van came round the dangerous corner there, on the wrong side of the road. He missed us by inches. Although he was in the wrong I fear it would have been we who would have suffered most. Ruth and I then walked on ahead, leaving Elsie so that she would get the first lift that came along as she was trying to get home as soon as possible. As it happened, we got the first one as a lorry passed Elsie and stopped to pick us up. It was pretty uncomfortable standing in the back but it got us to Taunton. On the way we passed a big van which we had seen in Bridgewater and which had passed us in North Petherton. There was a WAAF perched on the back amongst mattress looking articles. They were certainly full up and we wondered how far she had come and was being taken. In Taunton on the Exeter road the lorry stopped and he said he was going on to Exeter in twenty minutes time, but the few miles we had done in the back were enough for us!

Just as we were walking off, past the Municipal buildings who should we see behind this but Elsie. A small car had picked her up and a soldier who was also hitching. Very soon a big taxi picked us all up all the way to Exeter. Just before Wellington we had almost missed Elsie and the soldier, being rather intent on our new map of Cornwall. We were put down at the bypass and the other two went on into the centre of the town. The soldier was going to Crediton. He had done all the talking on the way down and we were all rather bored with him. It was very peaceful walking along the bypass, in the sun, eating our first bar of chocolate – peppermint cream. Just as we had finished kicking a stone for some distance, (a good way of passing the time but also of wearing away one's shoes), a

large car came along, stopped and off we went, bound for
Kingsbridge. The car had already come from Manchester
and was being driven to its owner at Bolt Head. We
gathered from the driver that the owner was rolling in
money and very generous. For my first time, I was taken
up the treacherous Telegraph Hill but it was like any other
hill to this large and powerful car in which we were
cruising at 45 mph. It was wonderfully comfortable and
one of the smoothest running cars in which I've ever
ridden. Alas! It seemed no time at all before we were
through Newton Abbot and nearly in Totnes, where we
got off at 10 to 4. Here Ruth posted a letter and we settled
down to wait just outside Baldwin's Garage. A strange
coincidence, that being Ruth's surname. We did not wait
too long before a milk lorry came along and away we
went to Plympton. The change of vehicle was amazing but
we didn't seem to notice much discomfort. At Plympton
we got, almost once a lift in a private car to Marsh Mills.
We could have gone all the way into Plymouth but had
decided to give the A374 Saltash Road a try. It was
certainly a stroke of luck, judging by the subsequent road,
that at that moment, a car stopped and we jumped in the
back. We were taken up over Crown Hill and down to St.
Budeaux which is the east side of the Saltash Ferry. We
walked a long way round to the ferry having been directed
wrongly but were fortunate in arriving, with a few
minutes to spare in time for the ferry. There are about 15
cars and lorries on the boat. One lorry offered to take us to
Callington but we didn't want to go too far inland. A man
and another one told us of a house in Carheal, just outside
Saltash, where we would get bed-and-breakfast so we
decided to take a lift on the lorry going to Callington and

they dropped us in Carheal. We decided to go to the house and when we had left our things to ring up my friend Barbara who had said she would be home that week. I was looking forward to seeing her after nearly 9 months. The room to which we were shown was filthy and the beds worse. In fact the whole place rather appalled but we felt we could hardly refuse now as it would soon be dark and at least this would be a roof over our heads. I rang up Barbara from the house to find she and her husband were on the Isle of Wight and not returning until the following week. Her mother remembered me from last summer when I had met her on the Island and said she would be delighted for us both to go down and see her. To cut a long story short Mrs. Ivory very kindly offered us a bed for the night most kind to us both Mr Ivory took me in the car to collect our luggage and when I returned two lovely poached eggs awaited me. We really did appreciate all Mrs Ivory did for us and I really felt that we hardly deserved it. We spent a most peaceful night and awoke to a very good breakfast and another lovely day. We set off again at 10 to 10 to see a bit of this Cornwall about which I had heard so much. Our first objective was to Looe but to get to it seemed rather difficult but we had high hopes so by about 11.15 we were there. Our lifts being one to Notter - only a few miles from Saltash and another to Landrake in a very dilapidated car. There we got one with a boy who I think should have had L plates front and rear. When we were dropped on the turning off to Looe from the A48 road, which we had struck south-west of St. Germans we very luckily got an open lorry nearly to Looe. Then a private car to East Looe itself. We had been told to go to Polperro but time was pressing so we crossed the bridge to West Looe and walked up to Port Looe from where we had a lovely view and I recognised the Eddystone lighthouse on the horizon. I have never in all my life seen sea so gloriously blue. The sky itself looked pale in comparison. Back in East Looe we made a big mistake. We accepted the offer of a lift up the valley way to Liskeard. Ruth sat in front and I was perched on the top of milk bottles, in the back with a very cheeky little rascal called Shirley. We were then dropped in the middle of nowhere at Plashford. We should have known better than to go that way but we felt that the driver should have known better than to leave us on such a deserted road. Having walked about 2 miles in the boiling sun we were just about at St. Keyne when a car passed us on a steep hill. We were glad when it turned out to be full. Just as we reached the top another car came along and stopped. Joy of joys they were going to Liskeard. Our luck was certainly in as they told us they don't usually come that way at all. Once more we made a mistake. We left the main road which we had taken so long to gain. In fact it was not entirely our fault as the man said he was going to Launceston. Then he put us down at Upton Cross, a good 10 miles from Launceston and once more in the middle of nowhere. We were at Upton Cross for a long time and were really feeling we would have to stay the night, though under which hedge we could not decide, none of them looked particularly inviting. I think we both prefer to forget the unpleasant time we had there, until nearly 4 o'clock, but it may have been just after. A GPO van stopped for us and he was able to put us down on the main Callington to Launceston road on his way to Callington. Just as we reached the road a private car stopped so we ran up and asked if they were going to Launceston. The woman, who had previously been driving changed places with her companion because she was only just learning to drive. They took us to within 3 miles of Launceston and then turned round to go back. We decided it was by now a little chilly so we put on our cardigans under our battledress tops again. Just as we had done this a car lept round corner on which we were standing and purely out of habit we put out our hands. It stopped at once and then we got on our last stage to Launceston, which had taken so long to reach. We sat on a ladder at the top of the hill leading down to the Okehampton road for about quarter of an hour and then I luck really changed at last. A large car whisked us off, not just to Okehampton but all the way to Exeter. We were warned that we would be murdered if we broke the eggs in the back so we were exceedingly careful. We had a most interesting commentary all the way on the odd villages and the Tors of Dartmoor. The Meldon viaduct was also pointed out, near Okehampton. At Exeter, although Ruth had suggested going by train we got a couple of buses nearly to the bypass. It was now just after six and we had quite a distance to cover before it was dark, which would be 7:30. We saw two of the men from camp with a car by the road but evidently it was someone else's which they were trying to start so that was not much good to us. Just then an open car came along and despite there being only one seat in the front, the back being covered with waterproof, the driver stopped. He took us to just beyond Broadclyst, Ruth sitting on my knee. Then came an enormous piece of luck. A few cars passed us and in watching them disappear round the corner we nearly missed one tearing along at a great speed. Luckily

Ruth saw it and put out her hand and we jumped in when it stopped. It was going right through to Wellington. The owner was an excellent driver and knew how to make the engine move. By 7 o'clock we were walking through Wellington and a few minutes later a bus stopped and picked us up. It was the one we had missed the previous Sunday by a few minutes. This bus got us to Taunton in time to have a most welcome wash and tidy before getting the bus to Bridgwater and so back to Weston Zoyland, which at times during the day we had had visions of not seeing until Monday. 231 miles

III

Stratford-upon-Avon to Overstone and Back

On Saturday April 13 I was staying in Stratford for my leave. I decided the night before to go to Overstone to see Margery. I looked it up on the map and found it was on the main road from Northampton to Kettering. On the previous day I had got a lift in a lorry to Warwick, when my Mother and I were going to Kenilworth and this lorry was going all the way across country to King's Lynn. It was doubtful I would get such luck again. I set off at twenty to nine and at once got a lift in a private car through Warwick to Leamington. We went across a bridge in Warwick from which I got a lovely view of the 14th Century castle which stands in amongst trees with the River Avon in the foreground. I had not long to wait before I got a lift in a big lorry to the crossroads a mile from Ufton and about three from Southam. After a few minutes I got into a van which was going all the way to Luton. To do this the man went through Southam and by-passed Daventry, with its wireless aerials and so on to Weedon where he turned off down the famous Watling

Street. I continued on the A45 in an Army lorry to the north side of Northampton. I am afraid this town did not appeal to me very much except the open part on the outskirts on the Kettering road. I had to wait a little while but then after some hesitation a private car stopped and in I jumped. He had not meant to stop originally as he was only going as far as Overstone and thought I would want to go all the way to Kettering. On the way I found he knew the Bremridges [Margery's family] and he took me along to their house. This was a very lucky lift as I would otherwise have had about three quarters of a mile walk from the main road. The family were all in when I arrived at ten fifteen. I stayed to lunch and tea and spent a very pleasant day with them. I left on the twenty to five bus. When I got to Northampton I had not too far to walk before reaching the Weedon road once more. There were a great many buses and bicycles so that hitching was somewhat difficult but a lorry soon stopped and I jumped up on the back with two aircrew bods. There was another airman inside. They were going to Birmingham and decided to put me off at the Coventry bypass. As I had no map with me this did not mean very much but they seemed to know so I trusted to luck. Just after Daventry we picked up some more airmen, incidentally from the same 'drome as the other two, one of which was making for Manchester and the other for Stoke-on-Trent. Then about five soldiers joined us but got off at Dunchurch. Just as I left them on the Coventry bypass a small private car with two women in front pulled up and they took me to Kenilworth. I knew the road from here having hitched back the previous day, when I had been lucky in getting a lorry all the way back. In Kenilworth I got a private car with a man and his wife to Warwick. They had lived at Cowes, by the aerodrome, for ten years, but now lived in Warwick. It was some few minutes before I could get one of the cars to stop. Even an RAF officer whizzed past without stopping but in the end I did very well. To the top of Black Hill, a few miles from Stratford I got a lift with a man in an almost unused 1939, eighteen horse power M.G. I would not have minded how far I had to go in her. Not long afterwards I jumped in the back of a tiny car and the two occupants said, 'Come and join the wreck' and off we rattled. What a contrast, but they got me to Stratford just before half past seven. I got back with a very light heart, knowing that from the next day we would be having an extra hour of daylight in the evenings. 99 miles

IV

Stratford-upon-Avon to Hook

Having seen my Mother off on the ten o'clock train from Stratford on Monday April 15 I returned to the hotel, got my haversack and at twenty to eleven set off to try to beat her. Her train was due in at Hook at a quarter to three. I soon got a lift in a small private car to a garage just beyond Alderminster, four or five miles from Stratford. Then after waiting a few minutes another car set off from the garage and stopped to give me a lift. He took me to the Chipping Norton crossroads, well on the way to Oxford. When we passed the signpost saying Great Rollright the driver told me that nearby was a miniature Stone Henge. He also told me a story about one of the stones, which is apart from the rest and only half way up the hill. It is meant to be a man who was a kind of Druid Chief but who had said, 'When Long Compton I can see, King of England I will be.' The point of the story being that he was then turned to stone and if one walks a couple of paces up the hill from the stone one gets a wonderful view of Long Compton, which could not previously be seen at all. Just as we reached the cross roads a car overtook us and stopped about a hundred yards away. An airman got out and very luckily for me the car waited until I caught it up. He was going all the way to Newbury, which suited me fine. From here onwards we passed through some lovely countryside, with rolling hills and gradually going down towards the valley of the Thames and into Oxford [shire]. We followed this valley until we had crossed into Berkshire and reached the town of Abingdon. In Oxford, we had a long wait at the traffic lights and a civilian woman came and asked for a lift to Abingdon and was even more pleased when we told her we were going to Newbury. I gathered from her subsequent conversation that she had been hitching this journey regularly all during the war. She even had the cheek to resent it when military vehicles sometimes refused to take her, which I thought was pretty good! But perhaps I should not be so hard on her. I would probably do the same if I ever had the nerve without uniform on. We reached Newbury at about a quarter to one and then I knew I had a difficult road ahead to Basingstoke. No hurry. Then along came a very nice little open sports model, an RAF Sgt driving and a F/LT with him. They pushed aside all the luggage in the back and in I hopped. Actually they were turning off at Kingsclere but in the end I turned off with them. They were off to Southampton for a court of enquiry, which incidentally should have begun at noon but they had been somewhat delayed en route, mainly by pubs I gathered! Now they were off the road and quite lost. They had come from Chipping Norton and had missed the turning at Newbury. As I had time to spare I went with them through Whitchurch until we got to Sutton Scotney on the A30 London road, where I left them. They were great fun and I thoroughly enjoyed my trip, which was through some lovely country. Not long after I had left them a big eighteen horsepower Wolsey stopped and in I got. I gathered he was in a hurry as we kept up a steady 80 M.P.H. My supposition was quite correct. He had an appointment in London at a quarter past four. He dropped me in Hook a minute after my mother's train was due, in other words just after a quarter to three. I walked down to the station to find her train was late, so I phoned for a taxi and just as I finished her train drew in. On that journey, at least, hitching certainly proved the quicker method of travelling and I had gone quite a lot out of my way.

V

Hook to Arundel and Back via Kingston

On Tuesday April 16 I decided to make the best of
another fine day and explore some new ground. I set off
from Hook just before ten o'clock and got a lift to the
Winchester bypass in a small army van with two civvies'
men. The back was packed with small square wooden
boxes with U.S.A.A.F. [United States Army Air Force]
instruments in them. I was aiming for Petersfield so when
we reached the crossing with the two bridges I asked to be
put down but they said that was the Alton road and they
took me to the traffic light turning. I soon discovered that
that was the Portsmouth road so I got a lift back in a
private car going up to London. I got out at a small
turning between the two but this was also wrong so I
walked back to the original place and saw that it was the
Petersfield road after all. My next lift was with a girl in an
M.A.P. lorry. She was going to Weybridge but if that was
the Petersfield road it struck me that she was on the wrong
road. Then I discovered that it was one and the same road
for some distance and then the Petersfield road branched
off to the right so I had to get off. Almost at once a big

eighteen-horsepower Austin came along. The owner, a very nice woman with whom I had a very interesting conversation, had come from Bournemouth and was returning to her home just beyond Petersfield. Instead of going all the way by the main road which takes the lower land we turned off to the right to Lane End Down up over the hills to Warnford. The view from here was good, but would of course have been better if there had been no mist. This mist, which turned to a heat haze, lasted nearly all day, rather spoiling several views. From Warnford we went to West Meon on the Alton- Fareham A32 road then across country again to East Meon. All these villages were very attractive and the new spring green everywhere added to their attraction. By now we had left the hilltops and were motoring along a green valley to Langrish, where we rejoined the main road and were soon in the little market town of Petersfield. I was put down at the turning to Midhurst, having come about a mile along the famous "Portsmouth Road". It was not long before a sailor, driving a big lorry, stopped and in I climbed. With some difficulty as the door was rather dilapidated. It was difficult to hold a normal conversation above the roar of the engine, but I gathered we were bound for Arundel. We stopped at a small pub just before... I had a shandy and he had a pint. It was then that I decided to go all the way to Arundel with him. The country we went through was lovely and was made so much better by the spring leaves just showing on the trees. I even had a glimpse of a few oak leaves. After a very steep climb with a glorious view behind us we drove down into Arundel. The castle there reminded me very much of the buildings in the film of Henry V. [Laurence Olivier. 1944. I will prefer the 1989

Kenneth Branagh one]. We parked the lorry and found a very nice little place where we had lunch. I only joined him on condition that I paid for my own so that everything went off very well. We had a jolly good lunch and then went down to Littlehampton on our way to Ford, where we delivered the lorry. They were all civilians at the M.T. Section and they were very kind to us and gave us transport back to Arundel. By this time we had discovered each other's name. The sailor's name was John. We did not have to wait long before we got a lift in a milk lorry to Billingshurst. I should explain that our plan was to hitch together up to London. John had to catch the night train back to Scotland from where he had driven the truck and he had intended going by a stuffy old train, but as it was such a lovely day it did not take me long to persuade him to hitch instead. At Billingshurst we got a lift all the way up to London in a very nice little open sports car. The driver was an ex-army officer who had only just been demobbed and as he had been overseas he had quite a lot of petrol and was using it to go round visiting his friends and relations. He came from Newcastle. It was a lovely run up to Kingston where I got off as I did not want to go right into town. It was only four o'clock so I decided to make for Guildford. After some time I got a lift to about half way to Guildford in a very big car. I asked about its make and size and was told it was a Hillman Hawk 23 H.P. We did a steady 65 M.P.H. but it felt like no speed at all. The driver told me that although he could easily get 90-100 M.P.H. out of it he could not afford either the tyres or petrol. As luck would have it I then got a lift nearly to Guildford in a 20 H.P. Daimler. This also was a very comfortable run and we were once again passing through lovely countryside. Then I got a ride to Guildford bypass in a small private car with a husband and wife and two small boys, both very shy. Almost at once a small R.N. van came along and the WREN driver stopped and I jumped in the back. She and the Naval PO with her were going down to Portsmouth. She evidently had a date at 6.30, when she got back so she was hurrying as much as the little engine would allow. I stayed in until Petersfield. I could not see an awful lot, but I recognised the country behind Haslemere when we went round The Devil's Punchbowl, where I used to ride quite a lot from school. [Oak Hall 1934 to 1938, following Munich] At Petersfield I had to wait quite a time at the level crossing but there was quite a good collection of cars, the last of which was a Carter Patterson van, into which I got. He rattled me along to the Winchester bypass. This was an interesting run as it took me on the lower and main road that I had missed in the morning when I went round the Meons. Just as I got to the bypass I was able to stop a lovely big and comfortable car with two men in the front. They were going all the way up to London at no small speed. They talked to themselves all the time so I had time to lean back and be quiet for a while. This does not often happen when hitching as everyone usually wants to know all about you and your views on the Services and demob etc., etc. [Everyone had a demob number but some were immediately exempt.] When we reached The Baredown [at Nately Scures near Hook.] they kindly drove right up to the front door and out I got at five past seven, just in time for a big dinner and then to bed feeling very tired but a bit more sun burnt and extremely happy.

VI

Hook to Lymington

On April 18 my official leave was up but I had an extra pass for the four days over Easter. I arranged to return to the Isle of Wight. Having had lunch at the "The Baredown" where I had been staying, at two o'clock I set off in a slight drizzle. The first car I got was an amazing coincidence. The driver was going all the way down to East Quantoxhead, which meant he would be going right through Weston Zoyland where I was still stationed. Unfortunately, of course this was not much help to me on this occasion and I doubt if I shall ever get such an offer again. At the Basingstoke bypass, I was lucky in getting a lift in a small private van to Winchester with a man who was going to pick up his wife and take her on down to Lymington. He was staying in Winchester for tea so there was no point in me going on any further. I soon got a lift in a small Fiat which was going to Portsmouth so that was only a short journey. Then I got in the back of a private car with a very foreign man driving and an English woman, who took me to Southampton. By now it was very cold and it seemed ages before anything stopped.

Even then I was only taken about four miles. Then I got a lift in a private car to Brockenhurst. The level crossing was closed so I went up to one of the cars waiting to cross and they agreed to take me to Lymington, where I arrived at a quarter to four. As the boat left at ten past four I had just managed things very nicely.

VII

Lymington to Bridgwater

On Easter Monday I had, unfortunately, to return to Bridgwater. I had had some most glorious four days on the Island walking, sunbathing, swimming and rowing. On Monday morning I went with the dog, on a canoe at Freshwater Bay and came back soaked through and I had to leave my slacks behind to be dried and sent on. I just had time for a lovely big lunch and ran to catch the bus to Yarmouth from where I went to Lymington once more in the ferry, but by now I was a very sunburnt and healthy person not the tired and weary WAAF who had gone on leave feeling very browned off only a fortnight previously. When I got off the boat I soon stopped a man going right up to Byfleet. I was not quite sure of the Salisbury turning at Southampton but saw it just in time. The weather was marvellous and of course there was a great deal of traffic on the road, especially going down to Bournemouth. Most of the cars were very full up, but eventually one stopped. I was not taken very far in that one but just after I had got out I stopped a milk lorry and he took me as far as... well on the way to Salisbury. Then

I had a stroke of luck and got a lift in a small private car with a man and his wife driving to Bristol. They had been staying with friends and were now returning after their Easter holiday. They had their old spaniel in the back and she was very friendly and did not seem to mind me being there at all. They very kindly took me up to Bedminster when we got to Bristol so I had not far to walk to the top on the downs. There I soon got a lift with a man in a private car who was going to pick up some people at Cheddar. I had only just got out on to the road when I saw a police car coming along. I did not put my hand out as I know they are not allowed to give lifts but all the same he stopped and in I got. He said that although he should not pick me up he could not possibly see a blonde left on the side of the road. Evidently my hair is the right colour for hitching – I have been told so on several occasions. He took me, not to the first turning along the top road to Cheddar as he said cars would not stop for me there, but right down to the bottom down the road I had gone along by cycle when I cycled from Bridgwater to Cheddar and back by Wells and Glastonbury. It was some time before I got another lift. All the traffic was streaming northwards after the Easter Monday and weekend rush for the coast and the 'Sunny South'. Eventually a car stopped and the driver told me he was going all the way down to Liskeard in Cornwall. He was a most interesting person to talk to and we had a long discussion on the proposed extensions of Plymouth about which I had read in the paper a few days previously. It was all very enlightening and finished off the day very well for me.

VIII

Lymington to Bridgwater

At twenty past twelve on Saturday, April 27 I set off from camp, making for Beer where I was to stay the night. I got a lift fairly easily into Bridgwater in a private car but we stopped for some time on the way while the driver chatted to a friend of his. He met another friend at the bottom of the town who very kindly took me up to the Taunton road. I had not been there long when two RAF boys came along and just then a little bus pulled up and in we got. It had the Air Force sign on the front but was empty except for the driver and one girl. The other two men got off at Taunton and I went on to Wellington. Although they were going right down to Plymouth I did not go all the way to Exeter with them as they were stopping in Wellington, for lunch and I wanted to press on. In Wellington I was lucky in getting a lift with a woman in a big car. It is only a few miles but it got me away from the built-up area where it is always more difficult to get lifts. Then I got a lift in a milk lorry as far as Waterloo Cross, where I had several times previously been put down on my return journeys. If I had just been hitching for the fun of it and had not been fussy about where I went my next lift would have been simply grand. It was in a small private car with two girls, one whom was an ex-WAAF. They were going all the way down to Helstone in Cornwall. At Exeter they went through the town and I walked along the bypass to the A35 road for Lyme Regis. It would have been quicker for me if I had waited for a lift on the corner but I had not realised then how far it was to walk. Then I had a couple of lifts to Sidford, the first one being only a few miles with a Flight Lieutenant who had come up from Cornwall and was very nearly home. In the second car we picked up another WAAF who really amazed me. She wanted to get to Sidmouth, some fifteen to twenty odd miles but she just walked along the road and made no indication whatsoever that she wanted a lift. I'm afraid if I'd been driving I would have taken it for granted that she had not far to go and could get there by walking. I had not been waiting long at the bottom of the long hill at Sidmouth when a private car drew up and the owner took me right along to the turning down to Beer 2 miles from the village. Even after this I got a lift to the top of Beer with a man who was going to Seaton. I usually have to walk which is rather disheartening at the end of a long journey. I got in just in time to hear the most interesting part of the cup final, where Derby beat Charlton. It took three hours and forty minutes. The quickest I've never done the journey. On Sunday evening Pam [Patricia's friend who was in the WRNS], who was also staying with Patricia had a taxi into Axminster, which I shared with her. We left at five past five and I decided to try to go either by Chard or Honiton. When the train had gone the taxi driver, Mr Osborne asked several of the cars parked outside where they were going. The very last one was going to Chard, which suited me fine. When we got to Chard it was raining, but not too hard. I walked quite a distance along the Taunton road and then got a very lucky lift in a small private car all the way to Bridgwater. We arrived at ten past seven so had certainly beaten all my previous speeds for that journey by doing it in just over two hours. As I had missed the seven o'clock bus to camp I had a good meal in the Continental and then got a lift back to Weston Zoyland.

IX

Uxbridge to Winchfield and Back

On my first day at Uxbridge, Saturday, May 11 I finished
on camp just after twelve o'clock and then hitched home.
It was not a very successful day as I went to Reading
where it would have been better to cut down to the Staines
road at Slough. I got several lifts to Reading and then one
with a man who was going to Virginia Water. I had
previously been that way from Reading, but it was a very
long journey and I only did it to fill in time. When I got to
Wokingham I got out and having bought some cakes tried
to get to Camberley. It was very bad from here and when I
got... I had to get a bus to Camberley. Then I got a lift in
a private car to Blackwater and another with a Canadian
to Hartley Wintney. I then had to walk to Winchfield and
I was very tired by the time I got there. I had a very
pleasant and quiet weekend, and on Sunday evening at six
o'clock I bicycled to Hartley Whitney and left my
mother's bicycle there to be collected. I very soon got a
lift in a private car to Blackwater. There was also a sailor
in the car who was also going to London. Just as we got
out an army staff car pulled up to give a lift to a couple of

soldiers. We got in, too, and when he had deposited the soldiers at Camberley we got going at high-speed towards London. He put me down at Egham and almost at once I got a lift. It was in a small car and we were driven along at a very slow speed. The driver and his friend were going up to London so they put me down at Slough. At Windsor we got a lovely view of the castle just before we entered the town. I had thought we would never reach Slough at the speed we were going and he was a very careful driver. Anyway we reached Slough and I got a bus along the main street to the Uxbridge turning. I soon got a lift there, in a private car. The driver took me right through Uxbridge to the turning by 'The Vine' to the camp so I was saved waiting for a bus or walking. It had only taken me two hours.

X

Broughton to Grange and Whitehaven and Back

I was stationed at Barton Hall just north of Preston for nearly 3 weeks in May. On my first Saturday there I decided to see all I could of the Lake District. I set off with just my Air Force handbag with toothbrush and soap and a few etceteras. First of all I went down to Preston and bought a number of new maps, including North Lancashire and the English Lakes. I left at half past three and almost immediately got a lift in a big private car to Lancaster. The driver was going on to Morecombe so he was able to take me right through Lancaster and over the bridge before he put me down. It was only a few minutes before I got a lift in a lorry. He was going to Lindale, on the other side of Morecambe Bay though it is not on the coast itself. He told me that if I went down to Grange-over-Sands I would doubtless get somewhere to stay. Just before five o'clock I got a lift in a private car down to Grange. It appeared to be quite a nice little town. I went into one of the shops to find where I would get a bed. I went to two houses but neither of them could take me.

Then I went into a café and had a very good meal of bacon and chips. It was here that I was told of a house which would probably be able to take me. I went to what I thought was the house but in actual fact it was owned by the daughter of the other one. Mrs Farrow fixed me up with a very nice little bedroom. I went to meet the bus after that as the lorry driver said he would be on this and if I had not found the bed he would be able to get me one in Lindale. He was not on the bus so I was not able to thank him. I was in bed very early and after writing several letters I went to sleep. In the middle of the night I got up and opened the window a bit wider and this was the only time when I was able to see the sea. The tide was miles out both in the evening and the following morning. The wide space of Morecambe Bay was just a big stretch of sands except for the narrow river. At half past nine on Sunday morning I set off once more after a good breakfast. I was very lucky on my way out of Grange as I got a lift in a small meat van to Lindale. I was set down halfway up the hill out of the village so I had to walk up to the top. It was then about ten minutes before I got a lift in a lorry to Newby Bridge. The driver was going on to Ulverstone but I decided to make for Windermere. It took some time to get a lift and even then, it was only about five or six miles. Then I walked along a bit and was just in time to get a lift in a car which is just leaving the hotel. The owner was very kind indeed and took me all the way to Windermere although he was really not going as far as Bowness. This was very lucky indeed because just as I got out of his car I was able to stop another one. The man in front said they were going through Ambleside so in I got. I soon discovered they were going to Whitehaven right up on the coast. It needed no second thoughts to decide that I would go all the way with them. We went by Rydal Water, Grasmere and Thirlmere to Keswick. We stopped for a drink here, but they were not open so we pushed on to Cockermouth. The road here runs through very different country after Bassenthwaite, and it is not by any means as lovely as that between Windermere and Keswick. In Cockermouth we stopped for lunch and then went on to Whitehaven where we arrived at two o'clock. I arranged with the two men and if I got stuck on my return journey if I was in Whitehaven at nine o'clock that evening they would take me back to Lancaster. It was some time before I got another lift and that was in a small car as far as Egremont. Then I got another lift but again the car was branching off so I only got to the turning off to Berkermet. Then I got a car which at first I did not think was going to stop. This car took me to Gosforth. Here my luck changed again for the good. Since I had left Whitehaven it had taken a long time to reach Gosforth, and I was beginning to doubt whether I would be able to make it. I very soon got a lift in a private car with a veterinary surgeon from Millom. This meant that I had a lift all the way down the coast. The driver was very interesting and knew the surrounding country pretty well. The nicest part was just after we had left Ravenglass and crossed the River Esk when we were able to turn back and get a lovely view of Muncaster Castle. It reminded me of the view of Warwick Castle which I got on my leave in April. [Chapter III]. At Silecroft I got out as I was told most traffic does not bother to go right down to Millom only to go up to Broughton. I began walking along the road running east beneath Black Combe. An odd car or two passed me without stopping. Then at last a private car pulled up and in I got. The occupants were a Father and Mother and their daughter, Julie. They were on their way to Ambleside which was marvellous for me. It meant a new road and once more through the Lakes instead of along the duller south road. They were very nice family and I thoroughly enjoyed my ride. They were very interested in where I had been and the conversation was very lively. The scenery by Coniston Water was lovely and when we reached the head of the lake we stopped the car for a while to get a better view of it. Then Julie and I between us guided her Father back to Ambleside by a different road from the main one by which they had come earlier in the afternoon. As we passed Bealham Tarn we feared we would not be able to see it, tucked away among the trees but we did get a very good view of it from one spot. It really looked almost unreal. At Ambleside we stopped at a café by the river and Julie's Father went in and bought us each a most delicious ice cream. We then had another one each as they were so very good. They then insisted on taking me to Windermere saying it was a pity I was not returning to Preston the following afternoon as they were going home then and would have been able to take me. At Windermere I saw an airman sitting waiting for a bus. He told me that what he thought of the people of Windermere could not be put into words. Evidently, he had not been as lucky as I usually am with his hitching. He seemed very disgruntled but was quite willing to get into the car which I soon stopped. This car took me to Kendal. The owners were going to Kirby Lonsdale but although I was tempted to go that way I decided to make straight for Lancaster. It was some minutes before I got a lift and I walked a little way out of Kendal. I felt fairly confident as there are not many roads leading out the Lake District and I think at weekends people from all the large towns and cities south of Preston go to that part and judging by the traffic most of them return on Sunday evening. When I did get a lift it was once more in a private car and the owner took me to Carnforth just north of Lancaster. When I got out of the car I got caught in the first shower which turned into a very wet evening. Fortunately, I only had time to put on my hat and put up my collar when I got my final lift in another car with a couple who were returning to Liverpool from Cockermouth. They were most surprised when I told them how far I had been. To conclude this most interesting weekend trip which, if it had been planned could not have been much better, a strange coincidence occurred the following evening. I had been writing letters in the canteen and walked up the road with them at about half past nine. I met one of the men on the course with whom I went into the local to buy some cigarettes for the other girls. As I was walking back having luckily refused a second shandy a car whizzed past and then suddenly pulled up and hooted the horn. It was Julie and her parents. It was certainly a very nice surprise and I was able to tell them I had got back safely and thank them once more for their part in what was perhaps my most successful weekend.

XI

Preston to Kirby Thore and Back

On the Saturday of my second weekend at Barton Hall I set out for Kirby Thore to go and see Ellie. [An old family friend] I got a lift down to Preston just before lunch and then at two o'clock I left Preston. The first lift I got from there was to a pub a few miles north of Broughton. Just as I got out of the car another pulled up and in I jumped. The driver was an ex-RAF officer who had been in for years and years. He was on his way to Lancaster and was going to spend the weekend fishing. Luckily, he was going right through Lancaster and so was able to drop me on the main Kendal road. It was only a very short time before a big car pulled up and I was taken in this all the way to Penrith. The occupants were a man driving, with his wife an Australian and their small son sitting in front. The wife was in the back with me and was most interesting to talk to. Although she comes from Australia and has travelled all over the world she still prefers England. Before the war she hitched with a friend of hers all the way across America. They were on their way to a little place called Alston on the other side of Cross Fell so after a glorious ride right over Shap they dropped me on the Penrith-Appleby road without going into Penrith itself. I was tempted to go up to Alston with them as it sounded such a grand little spot but naturally I was anxious to see Ellie so I got off. I had to wait some time before I got first an old car to a transport café and then a lorry to Kirby Thore. I arrived at half past four so I had only taken two and a half hours from Preston. Ellie was not in so I hitched back to Penrith and after buying a loaf of bread and having some tea I waited until she and her nephew David came to the bus stop. It was grand seeing her again and it was with great regrets that I had to leave at half past four. I walked a little way up the road and after about ten minutes got a lift in a car to Penrith. When I got out an RAF Sgt got out of a car from Carlisle and we waited together. He had done a lot of hitching all over England so we had lots to talk about. Not long after we got a marvellous lift in a NAFFI [NAVY ARMY AND AIR FORCE INSTITUTES] car with two men who were going to Liverpool. They were most surprised when I said I wanted to go to Preston. The Sgt got out at Kendal and was going on to Blackpool later on. He wanted me to meet him in Preston for the evening but of course I wasn't having any of that. We were lucky in getting that car as a big lorry stopped for us as well at Penrith but we saw the car first. Shap Fell by lorry did not amuse me at all. On the way out of Penrith we once more passed Lowther, the estate of the late Lord Lonsdale famous for his appearances at Ascot before the war. It is an enormous place and in a lovely part of the country. After Kendal we took the Kirby Lonsdale road for about ten miles and then met the other main road about eight miles from Lancaster. It was a pleasant change and a much quieter road than the main one which was absolutely packed as it had been the previous weekend. Once again the journey only took two and a half hours and it was still a lovely evening when I got back.

XII

Broughton, Longridge, Preston, Blackpool and Back

On Wednesday May 29, I set out at a quarter past six for a walk from Broughton House. I walked along the road towards Whittingham and Longbridge for a couple of miles or so and then an old couple picked me up in their car. They took me to Longbridge which I knew was all right as I could get a bus back. Having walked through Longridge, which was much bigger than I had expected I came to a café where I had two glasses of orangeade. The owner and his wife directed me down a hill and through some fields to get back onto another road. Very soon I got a lift with a man going to Preston. I had intended cutting across country to the north west but this lift was even better really. I was expecting a lift back to Broughton but once more fate had its own way and I was on my way to Blackpool. I had no idea of the time but the sun had not set so I thought I would be all right. We went to Blackpool by Lytham and St Anne's. It was a lovely run and I saw the sunset over the sea for the first time. At Blackpool I got a couple of trams out to the Kirkham road and was surprised to find that it was ten to ten. There were three airmen and a couple of soldiers already at the corner and the traffic was almost negligible. Then a big car drew up an airman and I got in. I would have waited my turn only it was getting dark and I did not want to be in Blackpool all night. The car was a big one and took us to RAF Kirkham where the owner dropped his son and the rest of us. I was very lucky and soon got a lift in a private car to Preston. I was lucky because by now it was dark. At Preston I stood under a lamp on the north side of the traffic lights and almost at once been an Army lorry came along. They were only going to Broughton but of course that suited me all right. I arrived back at twenty five to eleven which I considered pretty good from Blackpool.

XIII

Winchfield to Uxbridge, Lymington and Back to Uxbridge

After my course at Preston, I had a pass and went down to my caravan at Winchfield [In the Rectory garden with my mother's from where I would be married to Richard Hutchings on September 17 1949] on Friday, June 7. I had to be back on camp by nine o'clock in the morning. Luckily Alan was going up to Kew so we set off in his car at seven o'clock. It was a lovely run at that time of the day, with the road almost deserted. About three miles after Staines I guided him along the A315 road, which goes through Hounslow. This cut off a mile or so for him and he dropped me at Kew Bridge. I got a lorry along to Brentford where I was able to get a 65 bus up to Ealing. While waiting for a bus I got a lift in a private car to Southall. This was very lucky as the driver pointed out to me that it was much quicker to get a green line bus to Uxbridge than the slow train. This I did and was in camp at five to nine. In the evening I was allowed to collect my V-day and Whitsun pass so off I went again. I left camp at twenty to five and got a lorry to Hayes. The driver very kindly gave me an orange out of a big bag that he had. He dropped me at the traffic lights here and told me to go south rather than go along to Ealing. This was lucky because as I crossed that road I caught the eye of a F.Lt who was in a small open car. He stopped and in I got. He was travelling from Stratford-upon-Avon to Kingston so he was able to put me down on the Staines road when he crossed it. From here I got a lorry whose driver was going right down to Dorset and he tried very hard to persuade me to go all the way with him. At Hartley Row he stopped for something to eat and my luck was once more in. Another lorry pulled up and took me along to the Odiham turning by the Phoenix. Then I got a car to the station, a distance which I usually have to walk. When I had crossed the railway I then got a lift with a boy in a grocer's van right to the Rectory. The whole journey took two hours exactly. The next morning, I set off at about half past nine and began walking towards Odiham. I got a lift to the Odiham road and then after a while another to Odiham where I got a bus down to 'The Dorchester' on the main road. Almost at once I got a lift in a private car with a man and his very small daughter to whom I gave a bar of chocolate. There was quite a lot of traffic but most of it was holiday traffic and was full up. After some while I got a very good lift with a man who was going to Bournemouth. He had come down from near King's Lynn, having left early in the morning. He was very tired so was quite glad to have me to talk to to prevent him going sleep. We went by Winchester and on to Romsey. It was horrid weather – raining nearly all the time. He put me down at Cadnam and continued on his way. The first car that I stopped after that took me to Lyndhurst. The occupants were also going to Bournemouth but their AA route was a much more recent one than the one I had been following in the last lift and the route was via Lyndhurst and not Ringwood. It was quite a long time before I got a lift to Lymington in a private car with a man and his son. I was just in time for the ten past twelve boat. I was very glad indeed to be back on the Island once again though it was only until the Tuesday evening. For once I really did intend returning to London by train on the Tuesday but fate was against me. The boat was late and consequently I missed the fast train by a few minutes in Brockenhurst. The next one was in ten minutes' time (6.19) that meant changing and leaving Southampton to be in London by eleven something. That did not amuse me. Just after that train had left one of the cars, stopped by the level crossing gates now came to a standstill to pick me up. The driver a WAAF on demob leave took me as far as Lyndhurst where I decided to take the route by which I had come down on Saturday. My luck was in. A few minutes later a small car stopped for me and the driver took me all the way to Reading. He was most surprised that I wanted to go so far. Just as I was passing the General Hospital a car came along at great speed and the driver who was going back to a camp north of London took me about half way to Maidenhead. He was in a tearing hurry and I hardly seemed to have got in before I was out again. Only a couple of minutes later I got a lift with a man in a private car right to the gates of the camp at Uxbridge where he left me just before ten o'clock. If I'd waited for the train I would not even have been in London by that time. We stopped at the Blue Boar Hotel on the way for a drink and it was really a very nice place. I think it was just before Slough.

XIV

Blake Hall to Skegness and Back

I had nothing special to do on my first weekend at Blake
Hall so I decided to go northwards towards Cambridge,
which I had been told to go and see if I got the chance. I
left at a quarter past twelve and my very first lift was the
only one I had the whole day. It was a fairly comfortable
lorry and the driver was going all the way up to Grantham
so I went up there where we arrived at a quarter past six in
the evening. We went to Epping and then cut cross to
Waltham Cross and stopped at Cheshunt for a very good
salad lunch, with strawberries and ice cream. Then we
made for Stevenage and the Great North Road via Ware
and Hertford. From Stevenage It was just a straight run to
Grantham. We went through some quite nice country but I
did not like it a great deal. The best part was between
Stamford and Grantham where the ground is very
undulating and slightly more wooded than previously. I
was disappointed with Stilton not at all like the other
cheese village I had visited Cheddar, Grantham was not a
nice town and I could get nowhere to stay. If I had been a
man I could have got several beds, but the one girls'

hostel was full so I spent the night at the RAF camp. In the evening I went to the cinema and saw Bette Davis and Cornell Wilde in 'The Corn is Green' which I had wanted to see for some time. I left the next morning at nine o'clock and got a lift almost at once all the way to Skegness. The driver was so sorry he had arranged to meet people for the day, as he knew some lovely places which we could have gone for the day. Needless to say I was most relieved that he had other arrangements. We went through Boston with its 'Stump' to be seen for miles around. It was not surprising it had been such a good landmark for the Jerries during the war. The road to Skegness was very full and the going was rather slow, especially as there seemed to be no end to all the turnings and twistings. The countryside was terribly flat and would have been very dull if it had not been for the fields full of crops so much better looking and further on than any down in the south. It is certainly a wonderful farming soil. Skegness was very crowded so I decided not to stay long. I had a very good lunch and then set off back. I got one lift a few miles. Then another a few miles but then I had quite a long wait before I got a lorry and then I took a bus to Bolton as all the traffic was still going towards the coast. I walked through Boston and then got a lift with an ex RAF man who took me all the way down to Wisbech. It was a very pleasant journey. The heat was terrific but I thoroughly enjoyed it. From Wisbech I got a lift in a private car to Upwell where I had quite a long way in the hot sun. Then I got a lift with a couple just on their way home at Welney, only a few miles on. After a time I got a lift with a family, who had been to Hunstanton for the day. They gave me a few strawberries out of the big basketful which they had. By then I was, of course, in the midst of one of our biggest strawberry growing districts. The sun must have done a lot of good to them that day after all the rain we had been having. My next lift was in the back of a small car down to Ely from where a young boy took me to Streatham a few miles south. Then I had a real stroke of luck, especially after all those short rides which all the same got me quite a long way between them. A small private car stopped. It was occupied by a girl of about thirteen with her aunt and uncle. They were going to Chelmsford so were able to take me all the way and so to within about twelve miles of my destination. We came down by Cambridge, which I liked the look of and Saffron Walden. Parts of the countryside were very nice round there. From Chelmsford I got a lift in a big car going into London and the two men in it were able to drop me at the bottom of the drive at Blake Hall. It was a grand weekend and I really enjoyed every moment of it. I arrived back at five to nine.

XV

Blake Hall to Cambridge and Back

Having seen a little of Cambridge I was determined to see more of it. On the Wednesday following my weekend trip to Skegness I decided quite unexpectedly to go up to Cambridge in the afternoon. I got a lift to Epping and from there I went to Bishop's Stortford in a small private car. Just as it began raining a bit I got a lift in a lorry and at the speed at which we went we were very soon in Cambridge after quite a dull run up there. I visited several bookshops while I was up there and got several more maps, nearly completing my collection. Cambridge is a lovely clean and spacious town and I was most favourably impressed. I had no time to look over any of the colleges but I would like to go back there and find someone who will show me all over. I don't think I like any town as much as that one. My first lift out of the town was with a man going down to Windsor so I went along yet another road. We went through Royston and so down to Hatfield where I left him as I did not want to be too late back though I would have liked to have gone all the way to Windsor with him. At Hatfield, I got a lift to Hertford with a man who was most surprised at all my hitching and wished he had the time to do likewise. My next lift was most amusing. It was in a small car with an RAF Corporal who was on his way to Ongar from Cardington, where he had just been demobbed. On the seat beside him were three ice creams which he was taking home with him. It was fairly obvious that in the heat they had no chance of survival so in the end we ate them between us. We journeyed across country from Hertford so I was back much quicker than I expected which was just as well as I had a lot to get done that evening.

XVI

Blake Hall to Tunbridge Wells and Back

Two weekends before I went down to the caravan and
then down to Freshwater to see my new puppy, I decided
to go and see Aunt Nora [Cleland] and Aunt Greta
[Doxford] at Tunbridge Wells. [26 and 28 Broadwater
Down] That was on June 29. I set off just after twelve
o'clock and my first lift took me to Chelmsford. It was in
a big private car with an old chauffeur with a thumb
missing and a funny old man who spoke so softly that I
could hardly hear a word he said. It took me a long time to
find my way out of Chelmsford and I regretted not going
from Ongar to Brentwood. Anyway I did get a lift in the
end, to Brentwood where I waited about quarter of an
hour for a lift that took me at high speed right down to the
London-Southend road and there I was taken in a small
car right down to the ferry, which was a great help as a
boat was just due to go over. At Gravesend I walked
through the town and got on to the Wrotham road where I
got a lift to Wrotham in an army truck. My next lift was in
a private car with a man to Sevenoaks. I was a long time
getting a lift here and had to walk right up through the

133

town before I got a lift to Tonbridge. The countryside was simply lovely along the way and I decided that I definitely liked Kent. I got a bus to Tunbridge Wells and right up to Broadwater Down where I found Auntie Greta in her garden with my cousin Penelope Short in her WRENS uniform who unfortunately was not staying the night and left after dinner. The next evening I set off after tea and after a very pleasant weekend. I caught a bus to a few miles the other side of Tunbridge Wells. From there I was very lucky. I got a lift to Farnborough with the couple who were turning off there to go to Croydon. It was not long after that I got a lift right into London and was put down just on the south side of the river at... where I caught a bus to a tube station by which I went to Bow Road and by bus to Leytonstone at the 'Green Man'. Then I got my last lift in a small private car to Epping and I was back in camp in quite good time. The weather had been grand the whole time and I had had a lovely time.

XVII

Blake Hall to Stokesley and Back

[The home of Grandfather William Harkess. Shipbuilder and Mayor of Middlesbrough]

On the morning of Saturday, July 20 I suddenly had the idea that I would like to have a real shot at getting to Stokesley. I had been wanting to go there ever since I began my hitchhiking and if I had had more time I would have gone when I was up at Barton Hall. I set off from North Weald just before ten o'clock. My first lift was in the back of a small RAF transport which was going into London. I got off at the Wake Arms a few miles from Epping and did not have to wait long before getting a lift in a private car to Waltham Abbey from where I got a lift through Waltham Cross to Cheshunt. The driver was going due west so dropped me at the traffic lights on the more frequented main road. My next lift was in a lorry to Hoddesdon where I had a bit longer to wait before a car stopped at the garage for petrol and the man offered me a lift to Hertford, with his wife and baby in front and myself with their Scotty in the back it was quite a load. At Hertford I did not do so well as I tried to get lifts direct to

Stevenage. In the end I had to go to Hatfield first. This I did in a lorry until we got on to the Great North Road. At last. There was plenty of traffic and the first car I stopped was going to Northampton. When we stopped at the first garage I got out as I discovered that he would be turning off at the Welwyn sign so I might just as well get out now as later. It was just as well that I did that as just then a car pulled in for me and having been told I would be taken on up the A1 road I got in. It turned out that the driver was going to Lincoln over half way for me. I had reckoned that if I was in Grantham by three o'clock I would be on the safe side. Just after three I was put down at Newark, fourteen miles north of Grantham. We had stopped at a pub just short of Norman Cross. The driver bought me half a pint and we sat in the car eating sandwiches and wondering what it would be like with regard to getting those tasty morsels between bread after Monday when bread would be rationed. I only had time to walk down to the level crossing at Newark and wait about three minutes before I got the most wonderful lift I have ever had. My luck was certainly in. The car was a new one and the owner was going to York. It was a pleasant journey and on the way we made arrangements to meet at two o'clock the next day at the station in York as he was going back down to London. We could only do thirty MPH but all the same we were in York at six o'clock. [In those days new cars had to be run in] When I got out I was just going to walk along to a bus stop when I saw a car and thought I'd tried to hitch it. The driver stopped and took me to… which is about ten miles on the way to Thirsk. It was about five or ten minutes before I got my next lift because of course I was right off the Great North Road and traffic

136

had decreased accordingly. My next lift was in a large left-hand drive ambulance. It was a civilian one and was driven by a very nice girl. She was going to Northallerton but dropped me nearly in Thirsk. I was walking up to the village when out of a turning came a huge van with Redcar on it. Knowing it would have to go through Stokesley I was furious that I had missed it by so short a time. Only a minute would have made all the difference. Just after that an RAF car came tearing along and in I got. The driver was going to Middleton St George and was evidently in a tearing hurry. Anyway we very soon passed the big van and I was put down at a fork in the road just before Yarm. I went along the one marked Redcar and Stokesley and waited for the van. Then to my horror it went along the other way. I waited for some time and saw several cars go down the Yarm road but soon one came along my road and in I got. It was a pre-war German Opal, not very big but quite comfortable. The man and his wife were most surprised when I told them of my journey. They dropped me in Stokesley was just as the clock was striking eight. Stokesley who was just as I had remembered it and I had no difficulty in finding Aunty Mary's house. She was just coming out of it as I arrived and she was very much taken aback when I told her who I was. I got a tremendous welcome which was so grand after that long journey. I was whisked off to the cinema where I met Aunty Norah, Aunty Bee and Uncle Dick and it was not until one o'clock that I got to bed after a lovely supper and hot bath. [Bee and Dick had lost one of their twin sons in a Japanese POW camp. I remember them well as young boys. Norah and Mary were two of my mother's sisters. In WW1, my mother was in charge of

137

women munitions workers, Norah drove an ambulance on the western front and Mary was a nurse. Norah was the first woman pilot in Australia] In the morning I picked some lovely raspberries to take back with me and just before we set off in the car for York we each ate a bowl of rasps with milk and sugar. They were excellent. Aunty Norah came in the car and we set off about a quarter to twelve. Then a tragedy occurred at one o'clock or just beyond. The car refused to go any further. Luckily the first car that came along gave Aunty Mary and me a lift, Aunty Mary to the first garage for help and me to York. I did not like leaving them but it was imperative that I should get back to camp in time. I was in York a few minutes before two but had no time to look around it, much though I would have liked to, especially the Minster. Just after two we set off on our trip back. I discovered that this man was going nearly to Romford, which was simply marvellous. We were able to exceed 30 MPH just after Stamford as he had then done his first 500 miles. We stopped on the way for tea and also once for ices from one of the pre-war ice cream carts which one used to see up in the north. Just before Huntingdon we left the A1 road and went down through that town and Royston. Then my map came in most useful as I was able to get us up across country to Epping and then from there we went along to Blake Hall where I was dropped at about ten o'clock. That was certainly the furthest I had been in one weekend and that lift was most definitely the longest I have had so far. It was a very good weekend all round and when I got back it was hard to believe I had been so far.

XVIII

Blake Hall to Winchfield and Back

On Saturday July 27, Joan and I left Blake Hall at a quarter to eleven. We got a lift to Epping in a private car. After Joan had been to the Post Office I waited at the bus stop while she went and asked the occupants of an Air Force coach where they were going. That was the beginning of our luck as they took us round the North Circular Road to the Uxbridge turning. It was the Debnam coach taking the girls to the Inter-Command Sports at Uxbridge. Almost at once we got a lift to Brentford in a small Army transport. The driver wanted to drop us off on the A4 road but we were not going to get stuck on that. Not long after that we got a ride to Hounslow in a small private car and from there in another Army one to Staines. We were very lucky with this lift as there was a terrific downpour just as we got in which lasted nearly all the way to Staines. As we were waiting on the bridge a big RAF bus came along and stopped at the other end of the bridge for us. I was not too keen to get in it as I hate buses but we could hardly refuse. It was on the way to Black Bush and we were there in no time. After a few minutes, it then took us on to Hartley Wintney. Then we piled into the back of a heavily laden car which was going right through to Bristol. How we wished we could go all the way as they were going via Glastonbury, Wells and Cheddar. At Hook we had a good meal in the café and got some meat and rations and then got a lift in a van to Odiham, where we finished off our shopping and got a Camberley bus to the turning to Winchfield from where we have to walk. It is a lovely walk through the woods, but laden as we were we did not really appreciate it. We were very glad to relax in the caravan when we arrived. On Sunday we left the caravan at half past four and had to walk all the way to Hartley Wintney. It was about five minutes before we got a lift as most of the cars were full. Our waiting was rewarded, as the car we got was quite a fast one and we were taken up to the North Circular. Joan was going to go by tube from Osterley but decided to come on by road with me. We got about three or four different lifts round to Woodford, the last being with a man who was dashing down to Southend, having heard that his mother was very ill. We were chased and over taken several times by a very high-powered car with a stupid man at the wheel determined to show off to us. It slowed us down considerably, which was most annoying. At Woodford we had to wait some time, but in the end we got a lift in a small private car with a man who was only out looking for a drink. It was lucky for us that all the pubs were closed as it meant that he brought us all the way back.

XIX

Blake Hall to Isle of Wight and Back

On Saturday, August 3 I began my journey to the Isle of Wight in a huge lorry from which I was put down at the first roundabout after Epping. Almost immediately I got a lift in a small private car to Woodford. Then I got into another private car with two soldiers which took me well on my way round the North Circular Road. My next lift was very lucky indeed. It was in a privately-owned army staff car. In the front was an Air Force Sergeant who was on his way down to Reading. Then we picked up a soldier who was making for Weymouth. When we were put down, having travelled at high speed, at the first Uxbridge crossroads the soldier decided to go the Uxbridge way round. I do not know how he got on this time but if he had come with us he would I am sure have done much better. As we walked across the traffic lights I was able to signal a Naval van which stopped and took us from this to the end of the North Circular. After a few minutes wait an Army Captain in an open car stopped and in we got. He was going down to Dorchester but by Salisbury instead of Bournemouth as he expected engine trouble. Engine trouble set in just before Staines so after a few minutes we left him and at once I got a lift for us both in a car with a Wing Commander. He took us to… Then there was only room for one in the next lift so I went as I had further to go, but the Sergeant overtook me before we got started in a much bigger car. I did not see him again so expect he got home all right. That lift took me a few miles further on and I got another in a very rattley old car almost to Camberley. My next lift was with a man in a private car going down to Tavistock but I left at Hook so that I could get my rations and a good meal at the café. I got the good meal but alas I had lost my ration card in my pay book. I had no idea where I could have dropped it. Anyway I had to be on my way and my next lift was in a small car with the family going down to Burnham for their holiday. They put me down when they turned off to Basingstoke at the bypass. Not long after that a car with a man who was going down to Yeovil pulled up and whisked me off to the Wheatsheaf where I had hardly been out two minutes when a very nice car pulled up. I jumped into the back with a young girl who I think was the sister of the boy who was driving. In front with the driver was an Army Officer Cadet who was probably another brother. They were going to Bournemouth so took me all the way to Cadnam. Going through Winchester they had a special way of their own, which they said was much quicker. Just as we joined the main road once more the car which had been in front of us when we turned off rushed past which was really most amusing. At Cadnam I soon got a lift in a small car with a Guide Captain who took me down to Lyndhurst. I did not have time to walk far before I got a lift with a boy into Lymington. I was just in time to see a ferry go out so had to wait quite a long time on the quay for the next one. The boats were delayed a long time so I was very glad when an RASC motorboat came over with an Officer who let me and a Naval Officer to go back to Yarmouth. I learnt that evening that the ferry had had to stop and help with three boys and a man whose yacht had capsized. After a lovely weekend at Totland with Mr and Mrs Drake I had to leave once more on the Monday following but to Blake Hall I was taking two journeys, stopping at my caravan on the way for the Monday night. On Tuesday morning my first lift took me round to the beginning of the North Circular and then I got a lift to Finchley with a man who hadn't the use of one of his legs. For acceleration, he had an instrument on the steering wheel. Then I got a lift to Woodford where I was lucky to get a lovely big taxi to Epping. I was going by bus from there having met Miss Mann there but the bus was full so we hitched a lorry to North Weald and I got a car to Blake Hall.

XX

Penzance to Beer

Although there was a train from Penzance to Exeter at half past ten I decided on Sunday, August 18 to hitch to Beer as it was a lovely day. It was the end of my first Cornish holiday which in spite of indifferent weather I enjoyed very much. I left Penzance at about eleven o'clock and my first lift was in a small private car with two men. They took me nearly into… and almost at once a large car with two very nice people in it. The back was very full up but they squeezed me in on top of it all so that I was curled up and my head was bent to prevent banging against the roof. They were artists husband and wife and were off the day to the coast at… Wherever going to have a day off painting. They came from somewhere in the north I think and had just decided to extend their stay in Cornwall. I certainly envied them. After a few minutes they put me down. A small car rather full up with children stopped and they took me to the west. They were going on into the town but that would not have been much good for me. Almost at once in answer to my signal another private car stopped with a couple in the front. They were going right down to Fowey and I was very tempted to go with them, but in the end decided against it as I did not want to get stranded. Having bypassed Redruth they put me down where they branched off for Fowey and I continued my journey along the A30 road. After waking only about 5 minutes a small private car with a very nice girl in it gave me a lift. She was going all the way to Surrey but as she had to make a call at... beyond Launceston I continued on my own. I discovered that she had been in the wrens and had not long been demobbed. She had at one time been stationed at Cowes and knew Ruth McLaren [A school friend from Cheltenham who was in the WRNS] though not very well. Another strange thing too was that she had been staying at Lamorna Cove where I had been walking from Porthcurno to Mousehole a few days earlier. It was a lovely little place with only very few little cottages but a sweet stream running down to the small quay where they kept their few fishing boats. I had quite a long wait next but was rewarded at the end by a lift in quite a big car right through Okehampton and Exeter to within 2 miles of Beer on the main road above the village. The owner and his wife had been staying in Cornwall and were now on their way back to Bournemouth. Their son was somewhere behind them on a motorcycle but he did not catch us up while I was with them. Then I was spared the usual walk into Beer by getting a lift right down into the village. The journey took me just six hours.

XXI

Blake Hall to Willersey and Back

I had nowhere in particular to go on the weekend following my leave, so I wired Kay and asked if I could go down to Willersey half. The answer being 'yes' I set off at a quarter past ten on Saturday, August 24 determined to get to Cheltenham by hitching if it was possible. Then I could easily get a train from there. My first lift was in a large but very slow and old car with two girls. They hoped eventually to get right across, via Waltham Cross to... in... that would have been all right with me in a fast car as I would easily have got down from there to the Oxford road but I decided to go the other way. A car whisked past and then stopped about a hundred yards ahead so after running up to it I got in and they took me to Enfield from where I got a bus halfway to the North Circular Road and then a lift in a very dirty and smelly old dustcart with three equally dirty and smelly old men. I'm sure they were probably perfectly all right when not on their admittedly obnoxious job but it was difficult to bear with it. Anyway I then got on to the North Circular and got a lift straight through to the Western Avenue. The driver wanted Park Royal Standard works which I eventually found on my map and luckily it was just where the Western Avenue begins, so all was well. Then I got a lift for a few miles. Then I made a mistake. I got a lift in a lovely big car but it was going down to Hayes End and I went all the way instead of going on down the Western Avenue past North Holt. It was about twenty minutes before I got a lift to Uxbridge and then I had to walk right through the town and this took some time. My next lift took me about halfway between Beaconsfield and High Wycombe where I waited about ten minutes and got my best lift of the day. It was in quite a small car with a man from Derbyshire, who had come down to London that morning. We stopped at the... Hotel just at the bottom of the beautiful wooded hill that marks the boundary between Berkshire and Oxfordshire. There we had quite a good lunch after a couple of drinks and on we went. We missed the bypass at Oxford but with the aid of my map soon found it without retracing our steps. Then we stopped and the driver very kindly agreed, after consulting the map to take me to Willersey going to Stratford that way instead of by the direct route. I told him I could manage if he dropped me near Shepton Mallet but he was insistent. The day so far had been lovely but as we left Bourton the menacing clouds we had seen gathering were really falling hard and it rained incessantly from there onwards. It was a pity as the view from Fish Hill (or Broadway Hill as is its real name) is usually excellent. The Vale of Evesham and beyond can be seen to great advantage up there. I was put down at Kay's house at exactly four o'clock and the very kind man in the car refused even to come in for a cup of tea but I was most grateful to him for such a good journey. The next day Kay's brother took me on his motor bicycle down to Broadway and I left there at a quarter past two, laden with glorious Victorian plums and some tomatoes. After only a few minutes a big comfortable car with one man in it pulled up and in I jumped. He was fairly old and very quiet indeed and did not seem at all taken aback or either pleased or annoyed when asked if I could go all the way to London with him. The journey was speedy and very nice, with the exception that we ran over a lovely little bantam which should never have been allowed out in the road and also I felt a slightly strained atmosphere all the time. We stopped just after the… Hotel and went into a small but exceedingly nice little bungalow café on the right-hand side of the road. We had a light but refreshing tea there and then were passing North Holt in no time and just about four o'clock I was getting out once more by Park Royal. I then got a lift with a couple who [at this point there are six blank lines, except that I have written, obviously later in pencil Coney Hatch] My next lift took me almost to Woodford and I found it necessary to call at a nearby house to use their cloakroom. The woman there was very nice when she knew my need and offered me a cup of tea. But I explained my dislike of that beverage and was once more on my way. This time I was in a huge milk lorry going up to Ipswich with a rather nasty man who made suggestions which I did not appreciate so was relieved when he put me down at Epping where I very soon got a lift to Blake Hall, arriving back at seven o'clock.

XXII

Blake Hall to Lymington and Back

On the last day of August, a Saturday I set off from Blake Hall in the morning on the last long hitchhike for a long time. After that the days began to draw in so that it was dark too early to go far and in any case a week later I had to go home for a while for a rest in bed for several days and by the time I was well again, and had had a week on the island, winter was really here. My object in going down to the Isle of Wight on the Saturday was to collect Peter my black puppy one of the four which Mrs Drake's Buster had had on June 24. [The father being her son Bully!] By various stages I got on to the North Circular Road and as I was crossing the road at Woodford at the traffic lights a lorry signalled to me and I nodded my head and the driver pulled up. He took me a good way round and just in front I saw a car with the registration letters BOR and I remarked that perhaps he was going down through to Staines into Hampshire. [Our Morris car was BOR 10 before the war] I was very lucky when I got out as it was at some traffic lights and this car had stopped so I risked it and asked the driver how far he was going. His answer was very satisfactory it being Basingstoke. We stopped once on the way as he wanted a drink so after getting outside a pint he once more set off at high speed as his wife had a chicken for lunch and it was getting late. At Hook, he put me down and I went into the café there and had a very good meal, sharing a table with a civilian and an American GI. I was going to ask if they were going towards Southampton but as they began talking about Reading I left it and also I had no idea if they had transport or not. I went out before these two and saw a large American lorry outside and soon they came out and gave me a lift nearly to Southampton at quite a speed. I thought he was going almost into the town but he left us several miles out. The civilian caught a bus and I waited for a lift. An unfortunate thing happened on the way. We picked up a sailor and soldier and put down the latter at Winchester. They were in the back and although they tried to tell us we did not realise until we stopped that the sailor's suitcase had fallen out of the back. It was very bad luck as he had all his weekend things in it. I only hope he got it back the next week. My next lift was with an old gentleman whose granddaughter was in the WAAF and had done a lot of hitching. He very kindly took me right down to one of the main roads and from there I got a lift almost to Lyndhurst and then one into the town. From there I got a lift in a tiny little car with two old ladies who stopped when I signalled and wanted to know what it was I wanted. I was rather taken aback but managed to keep a straight face. They took me to the Brockenhurst where I soon got a lift into Lymington and I did not have long to wait for a boat. The next day I set off on an early boat so as to get back to camp before it was too dark. Peter [so named after my Aunt Evie's Old English sheep dog in Scotland] was very frightened in the bus to Yarmouth, never having left the house and garden before. He was very good on the boat and just as we were approaching Lymington I stepped out onto the car deck and asked the man and woman in the first car if they were going up towards Lyndhurst. It turned out that not only were they going up to London but the wife loved Peter so much that they very much liked having us. They did not know the way terribly well so I was able to guide them and save a lot of time. Peter was sick once but when we stopped at the Venture Restaurant on the Basingstoke bypass for lunch he slept quite happily on the floor of the car. Incidentally we had a very good lunch and I would not mind going there again. I was able to guide them as far as Piccadilly Circus but after that the wife knew the way so took over the directing. They were going down to... so they took me a long way towards Leytonstone. I got a trolley out there and then a very bumpy bus to Epping. By then poor Peter was definitely feeling not too good and I was relieved when I got out of the bus at Blake Hall with him safe and sound.

XXIII

Rudloe Manor to Roydon

Rudloe Manor did not impress me. There was no doubt about that and as the cold weather was just beginning when I arrived there on Friday, January 24, 1947 the result I was that I determined despite having only ten bob in my pocket to get home to Roydon somehow. Since my last hitching journey when Peter was only ten weeks' old a lot had happened including our moving our caravans to Roydon so that my mother could be near Blake Hall. During the winter months, it was no good trying to go a long way at weekends. Peter was not with me at Rudloe when I first went there. So I set off alone on Saturday the 25th just after twelve o'clock. First of all I had to walk down onto the main road but from there it was nearly all plain sailing. I first got a lift in a private car after about ten minutes' wait to the turning well beyond Calne which goes to Swindon. The owner of the car was just on his way to Rugby by a roundabout route to spend the weekend with his twin boy and girl and another daughter. We stopped once eggs and once for a dressed chicken and by the time we got there he had told me of how his wife had gone off and left him with the three children to look after. He also gave me a lecture on marriage – not the first time I have had while hitching. There was someone at the corner when I got there so I walked up a slight rise and round a corner. The first car did not stop but then I heard something coming very fast round the corner so got my hand all ready and raised it as a very dilapidated shooting brake piled high with antiques, even on the roof came along. I really did not think it would stop but it came to a shaky standstill not far from where I was standing. The nearside door was roped up with the ropes keeping the things on the roof. The driver got out and I had to squeeze myself between him and his passenger. It was rather a cramped position but as we tore along at between sixty and seventy miles it was not long before we were in Newbury having pulled up in Marlborough for the driver to rattle at the closed door of an antique shop but as he got no reply he did not bother. They dropped me on the London side of Newbury from where I got two lifts to Reading. I got off just before Reading, to be sure of getting a lift and sure enough I soon did. A huge great lorry pulled up and a couple of sailors hauled me on board. It was one of those that can hold a lot of people in front. I was freezing cold by now so was quite glad when we stopped just the other side of Reading and went into a very dirty looking shack where we had fried egg sandwiches and processed cheese. I was also ravenous so the food was most acceptable. As we progressed so I got colder and one of the men very kindly put his coat round my knees. I do hate having to wear tunic and skirt and not battle dress when travelling. It is much too cold in winter. After they put me down at the roundabout for the North

Circular I got various lifts round until I got nearly up to Broxbourne. Then, as it was getting late and even colder I got the bus and then a train which was just going. Altogether the journey was six hours but I was really glad to get home again even though it was only for one night.

XXIV

Rudloe Manor to Oxford and Back

Up to the time I went to Oxford for the weekend on March 15 the weather had been terrible. The snow and ice had made travelling by road almost impossible and had even caused chaos and havoc on the railways. The thaw was now setting in and the great floods which came had just begun. I had nothing to do for the weekend so I decided to get up to Oxford to see Anne. [Horsfall. I had learnt squash at her home in Andoversford on visits from school. Their car number was ADF 557! Her father had been in the Royal Flying Corps and had an aeroplane propeller. Anne was at Lady Margaret Hall. I would later meet her when playing Squash for Reading against Oxford] I had been once, by train but that had taken a very long time with a couple of changes and long waits because of the cuts of trains. I was not feeling too good as Peter had died two days before but I really felt I had to get away from camp. I set off at eleven o'clock on the main road with the NAAFI manageress and one of her girls. I got a lift in a private car to Chippenham. I walked out along the Swindon road and got a lorry after a short wait.

155

The driver took me as far as Wooten Bassett where I stood freezing for a while before I got a car a few miles. Then almost at once I got a mail van as far as Swindon. I got him to put me down before the town as I didn't know it well enough to walk through. Then I had what seemed to be an awfully long wait but I was rewarded by a lift in a big yellow car with a man who was going right through to Oxford. So far I had only seen one little bit of the flooding and that was the Avon just beyond Chippenham. As we approached Oxford there was another small patch just before the station but that was all. I got Oxford at one fifteen and surprised Anne who was sitting working hard in her room when I arrived. She had exams on the Monday so I left her to work while I went along to the G. F. S. hostel for my room. [Girls Friendly Society] When I went out there was a terrific wind and it was snowing hard. I had half expected it is they'd had a little in Bristol. I knew that as the man who gave me the last lift had come from there. When I returned to see Anne I was really wet and white all over. I had got some lemons in a shop and also my rations so we settled down for a lovely tea with hot, sweet lemon drink. After tea, I read while Anne worked and then we set off to the Stowaway the supper. The snow was thick now and also when we returned. Imagine my surprise when I woke in the morning to find the roads all clear and no snow anywhere. It had rained hard all night. Anne was away for the day so after getting the paper and going to church I sat in her room drinking more hot tea. At three o'clock I left Oxford as I had decided to hitch back as well. The papers were all full of flood news so I was not surprised to see a notice of 'Roads Flooded diversion for the Abingdon Road'. I'd not gone far after the station when I saw the floods. There was only a single line of traffic creeping through and lots of sightseers standing round watching. I had to get across the floods by stepping stones – once more only a single line so to meet anyone was rather a mishap. Fortunately, I was all right in that respect. I had my eye on the lorry so stood on the other side of the water for about ten minutes waiting for it to get through. When he did he took me as far as Farringdon. We had to negotiate about five more patches of dirty swirling water before we were clear of Oxford but we got on better than the smaller cars which had to go slowly for fear of splashing their engines. Before we reached Farringdon, it was raining hard but it had slacked off a bit when I have to get out. By this time the wind was getting up for the great gale which ensued that night when rooves were blown off and trees all over England were uprooted, including the one which fell within a good few yards of our caravans in Roydon. I got a lift to Chippenham from Farringdon in a small car with a man who the day before had gone from Bristol right up to Luton. What a wonderful lift that would have been had I been going home. We met no more floods till the Avon. When we got there the wind was lashing at the car and doing its best to put us off course. We saw no one about near the floodwater except a car the other side and a farm labourer on a bicycle. The driver decided to risk it and consequently we got stuck in the middle. It is a most peculiar feeling to be stuck in a car in the midst of muddy water with the engine gone quite dead. We really were very lucky as the farm man who, judging by the smell of his coat was a milkman very kindly pushed us to the other side where after a few seconds the engine started like a bird. I was not in time for the quarter past five bus so I stayed and had a meal before returning to Rudloe. By the time I got there the gate had begun in real earnest and I was glad not to be outside – though later that night, three of us had a taxi down to Chippenham to take a dog to the vet. What a journey!

XXV

Rudloe Manor to Roydon

The week after my trip to Oxford I rang my Mother up on the Thursday and she told me about the tree which had crashed down on the Sunday night. She said she did not think I should come home as the floods were so bad. By this time the Great North Road was impassable in most places. The Fens were flooded and Reading, Oxford and Maidenhead were several feet underwater to say nothing of the West Country, Wales and the Midlands. I told her I'd get home if I possibly could and she sounded very pleased about it. On Saturday I set off early at ten o'clock. I could have gone earlier, but we had another terrible downpour of rain into which I did not relish going. My first lift was a lorry to Chippenham and here I had to make my choice. Was it to be the awful cross country route by Oxford or should I risk Reading and Maidenhead? Luckily I decided the risk and was well rewarded. After a lift for a few miles I got a lift in a Vauxhall fourteen all the way to London. The owner was dashing up to meet his sister from America and I was glad he was in such a hurry. Reading itself was clear though in the distance I could see stretches of water. Then we had to go through Wokingham, Ascot, Egham and Staines. There was still three feet of water at Maidenhead. We made very good time and he dropped me off round the North Circular at Neasden. At Egham there were a few inches of water on the road, but across the fields only half caravans were visible above the water and a couple of feet of lamp posts and just the top part of an Inn sign. Until one saw that the floods were not the real thing at all. Even now it is hard to conceive the havoc wrought by them and the disaster that has come to so many homes especially I think in the fenlands. From Neasden I got a lift with two men to Tottenham where they put me down on the Cambridge Arterial Road. I had a bit of a wait there but then a man came and gave me a lift up to the Enfield Highway where a couple of Hertford Green Line buses were waiting but I left them and got a lift with a policeman up to Warmly where the two main roads run together. Almost at once I got a lift in a small private car with a couple and their boy, who were off to Bishops Stortford. This meant they could drop me at Stansted only a couple of miles from Roydon. I walked from there and arrived in record time at three fifteen.

XXVI

Rudloe to London and Back

I had a big stroke of luck on the weekend of March 29. I
was originally going home on a forty-eight hour pass on
Friday but had to play hockey at Uxbridge on that day so I
set off on Thursday. This suited me fine and I sent my
mother a telegram to say I was coming. I set off on the
half past three bus and got off after a couple of miles at
Corsham – on the main road. It was raining but that did
not worry me a lot. Almost as soon as I had finished
putting on my great coat a small car stopped and in I got.
The driver was a commercial traveller and was on his way
to Reading. He was most amusing and between us the
journey went very quickly. We stopped in Marlborough at
the Polly Tea Rooms and had a good tea and then off
again. Most of our conversation was about food as we
found here a common liking, I was feeling horribly
hungry by the time he put me down at about six o'clock
just before Reading. He was rather anxious that I should
get a train but I said jokingly that I would get an
enormous car when he'd gone and would soon be in
London. It seems to pay to have complete confidence.

Almost before he was out of sight a large Rolls-Royce came along and the ex-WREN who was driving gave me a lift all the way to Bayswater. I had not got time to catch the seven thirty train but I easily got the one after eight which is a fast one and I was home just after nine o'clock. After a very nice weekend and quite a strenuous one too I went to play hockey again at Uxbridge on Monday. This had meant Sunday night at home too, which was really wonderful. To save going right up to Paddington and then all the way down again I decided to hitch back to Rudloe after the match. I left Uxbridge at half past four and got a lift to a place a couple of miles on the Maidenhead side of Slough. After a few minutes I got a lift with a man to Reading. He was not going into the town so dropped me when he turned off. Just then three cars were coming along so I put out my hand and the best stopped. It was a forty-five horsepower Lagonda 1939 Model. The chauffeur who was driving it said he was going down to Hungerford which suited me fine. It was a lovely journey but would have been even better with no other traffic on the road. I had quite a wait at Hungerford but was once more rewarded with a Jeep this time. The army driver had a date in Marlborough for which I gathered he was late. We tore along at sixty nearly all the way. Luckily I knew the road at Marlborough as he told me the wrong one when he put me out just where the town begins. After a time I got a lift in a private car with a man who knew all about hitching. He used that method of transport while in France during the 1914/18 war and proceeded to tell me all about it. He also knew how to make his car move in spite of its age and state of decay. We were very soon at Beckhampton where in January I had got the lift in the 'antique' shooting brake. I had a longish wait here and in the end got a very slow, nasty little car with a smelly dog in it but it got me to Calne somehow, I was able to make myself fairly comfortable in spite of a large oil drum where my feet should have been. I was beginning to think about a bus when a lorry came along and in I got. I was dropped at Rudloe at about quarter to eight when it was still light. If I had gone up to London and got the train it would be nearly an hour later or even after that if I had missed the train.

XXVII

Rudloe to Roydon. Twice

This year I decided to have my seven days Easter leave in the week after Easter as I was sure the weather would be better. Incidentally that turned out to be true but that is beside the point. I was still able to get off for Easter Saturday and Sunday. I set off from Rudloe at about ten o'clock and did not do at all well that day. I got a lift almost to Chippenham and then had a long time to wait before I got another. With this second one I got to Calne and there I had another wait though not quite so long this time. My next lift was with a couple who were going to Guildford. I did not go with them as far as I could as they stopped at Savernake Forest to eat their sandwiches. I walked on several hundred yards and then got in quite a small car with a couple in front and quite a large woman behind. There was just about room for me. They were going through Wokingham so were able to drop me the right side of Reading. I had several minutes to wait before a large – rather dilapidated car pulled up and the owner – a Welshman took me and three army types to Slough. He dropped us before the town at my request and I had a long wait. The other three walked on and when I overtook them they were in the middle of the town. How they thought they'd get a lift there I don't know. The car we were all in seemed liable to give up the ghost at any minute and backfired most of the way. Then I got a lift with a man who was in some local office near Reading where they have been dealing with people in the flooded areas. He told me of all the cleaning that had to be done to all the flooded houses and how dreadful it had all been. What it can have been like in the Fenlands one dreads to think. When this man left me at the bottom of the North Circular Road I soon got a lift with a man as far as Park Royal. There I got a lorry as far as the turning off to Tottenham and in a very short time got a very nice lift. It was in quite a small and certainly not new car. The occupant did not look particularly inviting – in having orange coloured, wispy hair and a terribly freckled face. My first impressions were of an overgrown schoolboy. I got quite a surprise when he spoke as he had a very nice voice and was obviously well educated – appearances as so often can be deceptive. He was going right up through Broxbourne but it escapes my memory as I write now – a month later to the day for where he was actually making. It was some distance on and as he was not very familiar with the road I was able to help a little. The trouble was that I was still uncertain as to which road was the best way when leaving the North Circular. Now I believe I have solved the problem but even so am not absolutely sure. At Broxbourne I got a bus to Stanstead and then having walked to the top of the hill outside the village and with the thought of a mile to walk to Roydon a car came along and with great joy I was taken down to Roydon. It's often those short but sweet lifts at the end of a journey which seem to count so much more than the others. I am always so pleased when I have been prepared to do the tedious walk when someone takes the trouble to stop, as I don't like to put out my hand only to be taken a mile or so. I had a lovely Easter weekend with Mummy in our caravans, it being so much nicer than it might have been as it was so unexpected. I had to return on Sunday night, April 6 by train but on Easter Monday on a sudden impulse having nothing better to do, I decided to go back to Roydon to see Mummy. As I got outside the gate just after ten o'clock at Rudloe a car with two men in pulled up and whisked me straight off to London! They dropped me at Marble Arch at one o'clock and I got a Green Line out of London. Then I got a lift to Broxbourne but decided that as time with so short I'd ring Mummy up and she came and fetched me. The men who had given me a lift to London arranged to take me back if I was at Paddington between half past five and six and I thought I could be but as luck would have it, the 4.19 train was not in operation so I had to get several lifts down to London and must have missed them by about ten minutes and I had just time to get the 6.30 train and avoid all WAAF SP's, having no pass!

XXVIII

Southampton to Rudloe Manor

My Easter leave began on the third day following Easter, and I spent a lovely weekend down on the Island. The weather was really glorious, and when a telegram recalling me to camp arrived on the Monday morning my fury and disappointment were great. There being no explanation I naturally wondered what I'd done wrong but as it so happened I could not think of anything. Little did I know that this journey was the beginning of a fortnight's travels that took me nearly a thousand miles by road! I really had meant to get a train from Southampton, but as I was there at half past twelve and there was no train until nearly half past three I decided without hesitation to hitch. It had promised to be another perfect day when I left the Island as there was mist lying all round, which was gradually clearing. It was quite a while before I got a lift out of Southampton to Totton where the Salisbury road joins the other one. Then I got a lift in a large car to the turning off to Andover. I had another wait then, in which I discarded my greatcoat, as the sun was, once more really grand. Then I got a lift in a car for a few miles to a garage and a woman took me after that for another few miles nearer Salisbury. From there I got a lift with another woman into Salisbury. The previous one was a younger woman and her small fascinating daughter Cherry sat in the back of the car – very silent. In Salisbury I had not a long walk to get through and got a lift in a huge car with a man whose taxi it was. He ran me up to Warminster and told me of a shortcut by the churchyard to get through the main street. I was no sooner back on the main road than a car pulled up and two dear old ladies asked if I would like a lift. I sat with the chauffer in front and they were most surprised – and delighted to hear I was going to Bath. They took me all the way but as we approached it was all too obvious that on my return I was bringing rain with me. I was lucky in Bath as I got a lift with a man who, although he was only going about half way, ran me all the way up Box Hill to Rudloe, perched on the top. It really was raining hard when I arrived.

XXIX

Rudloe Manor to Kirkby Thore and Back

After one day of work at Rudloe I set off once more on what proved to be a very nice four days though at the start they seemed doomed. Maggie and I had to go up to Wilmslow to see if they could persuade us to become drill instructors. Heaven forbid! Wednesday April 16 was not a particularly nice morning for setting off to that city of rain – Manchester but at nine o'clock Maggie and I set off determined not to let anyone in the world dishearten us. Our first lift was in an old, small car with a man who took us down to the Gloucester road just before Bath. Here we were very lucky as we had not long to wait before a large car stopped and we were taken by a Scottish commercial traveller to Stroud. Maggie tried to persuade him that she needed the tweed costume he had but unluckily there was no response at all. The mist was thick going up over the hills but cleared as we got to Stroud. We could not decide at which corner to stand but having waited for some time at one we stood so that any traffic would see us and almost as we moved to our new position a milk lorry came along and took us over to the A38 road. It was a real blessing to see it as it was to take us as far as Birmingham and also I was on ground that I knew from days gone by. After five minutes' wait two cars pulled up together. The drivers were friends and we each got in a different car and were taken to Gloucester. This was of course after the Budget – that well remembered one, as I am sure it will be, when cigarettes went up to 3/4d. Most of the conversations we had that day at least touched on the subject and in the second lift we had Maggie solemnly smoked her last cigarette with our Scottish friend. The fact that she still smokes has nothing to do with this story and is quite irrelevant! In Gloucester we found a little café, not clean or nice, with nothing to eat but at least we could spend a penny. A great difficulty on such a long journey as one never knows where one is likely to get put down next. Our next lift was a very hurried one to Tewksbury in the back of an army 15 cwt with a Scotsman. In Tewksbury we resisted the temptation to have lunch. We decided to do this after <u>one</u> more lift. We walked out of Tewksbury and just over the bridge where, although the river was many feet below the board giving the 1947 Flood Level was half way up the railing along the road. Several had given way altogether and a few boats had been left high and dry at ridiculous angles and in most odd places. Very soon we got a lift in a big lorry. He was going to Stoke and actually we'd seen the lorry in Tewksbury but hadn't known where the owner was. It was really quite a pleasant journey in spite of it being in a lorry. We stopped once on the way at a small hut type of transport café. There we had lovely Spam sandwiches with new bread and of course the other two had the usual cups of tea. At... the driver stopped the lorry and went across to the 'Gentlemen's'. We asked him if there was a 'Ladies' as well. He said yes but we couldn't find it so we made a dive across the road to a hairdresser's where they obliged us. It was just after four o'clock when we were put down on the north side of Newcastle-under-Lyme. Almost at once a smaller lorry stopped and he was going through Wilmslow to Manchester. Not long before Wilmslow we stopped just short of the little village of... and went into a small, but clean and nice cottage. There we had some lovely home-made cakes and could have had a very good cooked meal if only we had realised our driver was not in very much of a hurry. We decided that if we were at Wilmslow long we would go out there one evening. At last we arrived – at half past five and at once began recalling our separate stays at Wilmslow when we had each joined up three years previously. At about half past three the next day I was once more on my way. They had only wanted us for an interview of a few minutes so Maggie set off by train for Winchester, with the return railway warrant and I went on up to Kirby Thore to stay with Ellie. I had quite a long wait before I got a lift with a very nice couple who took me through Altringham. Actually they dropped me just in the wrong place but I was lucky in getting a lift almost at once with a man who took me to Sale. There I got a large car but the chauffer driving it said he was going to Manchester but he was able to take me a few miles to the turning at Seaforth [possibly Stretford] Once there I very quickly got a lift in a lorry going up to Burnley and they were able to put me off on the main Manchester – Chorley road. I walked a few hundred yards and waited for a while and was rewarded in getting a lift right up to and through Preston.

This saved a lot of time, as Preston is too big to get through quickly. I was put down outside a restaurant – just short of Broughton House where, last year I was billeted when on my EVT course at Barton Hall. From here onwards therefore I knew the road fairly well as I had been up to Penrith when I was there. I was quite hungry so stayed for a while and had a very good meal, plaice and chips followed by a trifle. I also had some delicious cocoa. As I left the café a lorry hooted at me and in I got. The driver took me up through Lancaster and although he was going to Milnthorpe I got him to drop me a little before that on a deserted piece of road. It was some time before I got another lift. Several cars and lorries passed. I was very lucky then as I got a lift in a private car with the Scotsman, who was going to Dumfries. We stopped once on the way and had an odd drink and then the rest of the way he insisted on singing to me. He also told me of various service people to whom he had given lifts at different times and his last remark when he left me at Penrith was that I must be sure to write to my mother and let her know I had arrived safely. He sounded most concerned in case I should forget. Almost at once a big police car pulled up and took me about halfway to Kirby Thore when we met his boss who was evidently giving the Vicar a lift. We two changed places and the two cars turned round and I was taken all the way to the Eden View Cottage where Ellie and her sister Ettie were most surprised to see me. After a lovely few days at the cottage I once more had to make tracks for Rudloe on the Sunday. I set out full of confidence though how I really thought I would be to do that all in one day I do not know. I had to walk quite a long way before I got a lift for about 2 miles with the district nurse. I had been hoping all the time that a large lorry parked outside a transport café up the road from Eden Cottage would pass me and was overjoyed when I saw it coming. Unfortunately for me the driver did not stop and I saw the reason why as he passed, there was a woman already in front with him. After another long walk at long last I got a lift in a lorry to Penrith. The driver had hoped to have my company all the way to Glasgow but of course I had to go the other way. As I jumped from his lorry at the corner where the Kirby Thore road joins the A6 another huge lorry stopped and much though I would rather have waited for a car I could hardly refuse the lift. In doing this I made a great mistake. Never have I met such a pessimist in all my life. He was going to Brum and would get me there by eight in the evening. He held out no hopes of getting there quicker and according to him lifts after that would be out of the question. We crawled up Shap and I hated the journey all the way over. At the Jungle Café on the other side which we seemed to take hours to reach we stopped and helped by an AA man I got myself a lift on a smaller lorry carrying wood. There were two of them and we went at a much better speed from then. They were actually going to Preston but at one o'clock they decided to stop for lunch but as time was marching on I did not like to stop and so walked on a couple of hundred yards down the road. We were then about halfway between Preston and Lancaster and having been with the pessimistic lorry driver, I really had my confidence in myself slightly shaken but not completely by a long way. Almost at once a small private car came hurtling along and stopped in answer to my signal. At last I felt I was getting somewhere. We rushed down to

Preston and through Chorley and though he was going through to Manchester I left him where I had left the lorry a few days ago on the main road south of Walden. After a short wait, I got a short lift to Bath Bridge and from there another short one to Stretford. Here I had quite a long wait and it really seemed to be getting late but I had no fears at all of not getting back on time. My confidence was rewarded at this point and all my subsequent lifts were not only fast but also over long distances. I just had one short lift to Altringham and it was round about four o'clock. I had walked a little way out of the town and was hoping any car that *did stop* would not be going through to Chester. I was lucky. A large Chrysler pulled up and in I got. There was a man and woman in front and they said they were going right down through Knutsford to Newcastle-under-Lyme – about thirty miles. They drove quite quickly but we were driving straight into a terrific downpour of rain. They had to turn off just before the town which was just as well for me. They were concerned about me getting wet but I assured them I'd soon get a lift. It may sound like sheer bravado was actually it was no such thing. I really believed a car would come along at once and rescue me from the storm and the amazing thing was that it happened. No sooner was the Chrysler out of sight than a smallish car came tearing along and slid to a standstill when I put out my hand. I had to creep in very quietly at the back as a small boy was asleep on his mother's knee while his father drove nice and fast all the way to Coventry. It was difficult to talk in whispers but we had to as I wanted to get off before I was taken off the beaten track. It was a question of Coventry or Wolverhampton and they persuaded me that Coventry would be just as good. At Stone we turned off for Rugeley, Lichfield and Tamworth thus leaving Birmingham well to our right. Then we cut down to Coleshill and they left me near the Coventry bypass on the road for Warwick. My luck held once more. On the opposite side of the road a couple had stopped for petrol and when they had carefully arranged for someone to have room to sit in the back they called and asked me if I would like a lift. Imagine my joy and relief when they said they were going to Bristol. That journey was the liveliest. The girl drove at first and quite recklessly. Unfortunately, they were following some friends who were liable to break down otherwise we could have gone down via Stratford where Mummie and Patricia were staying. At Cirencester we stopped for a few moments and the man took over the driving. I think he was really the better driver but also the more reckless. We tore down towards Bath at an incredible speed. Having struck the Fosse Way about 5 miles north of Shipston on Stour we left it about a mile south of the Thames Head to continue on its straight way across country to Bath. The main road follows the line across the southern tip of the Cotswolds where the old Roman road keeps to the lower route – at several places forming the boundary between Gloucestershire and Wiltshire. They left me at the Cross Keys Inn where they had to turn off for Bristol but I got a lift almost at once with a man and girl who I imagine were going to Bath for the evening. They put me down just outside Bath in time to get a lift with a taxi just going up to Rudloe. I was back on camp at ten past nine and it seemed hard to believe that only twelve hours before – the same day in fact I had been nearly three hundred miles away at Kirby Thore in Westmoreland and I had been through nine counties.

It is surprising to me when I realise that I only went through seven on my way up! I did not go through Warwickshire and as I did not actually have to go into Penrith to get to Kirby Thore on the main road. I did not get into Cumberland but only by a few yards. (Number of counties and last eight lines added November 21, 1949 M.E. Hutchings. This was two months after my marriage to Richard in the Norman church at Winchfield. In 1967 our market garden in Newchurch on the Isle of Wight would be called Winchfield Gardens. After I had given a talk to the Sandown Horticulture Society a man in the audience said he had always wondered why it was called Winchfield. He had been a porter on Winchfield railway station before the war. Our Hook station was the next one down the line from Waterloo.) This was the last hitchhike written up but here are the titles of four unrecorded ones. Rudloe to Stanstead Winnersh to Rudloe Winnersh to Roydon and Back Rudloe to Droitwich and Back. This one could have been to meet Aunt Evie Short who lived between Kelso and Yetholm in Scotland. Maybe she was taking the waters in the spa town.

Notes 1. I discovered in 2015 that it should be Westonzoyland but have left it as written in this book. 2. The word lucky appears 16 times in Book 1 and 51 times in Book 2. When I came to live in Freshwater Bay in 2004 it became apparent that 'luck' was still with me, but I named him Dippy, derived from Serendipity the ancient name for Ceylon/Sri Lanka where Richard was born in

1922 and where we cycled for a month in 1950 on our way to New Zealand. Birthplace of our three sons.

Richard diary extract

Richard having been taken ill with gastro enteritis he had been left behind when his unit in the Royal Signals had moved on. His hitching to try to catch up with them is recorded in his Diary 3. To find the story of his determination to creep out of hospital. I have found it all among poems, etc. I well remember a good time camping on the river bank at Pacy-sur-Eure. I have my only copy of many of his poems found in his diaries. hand bound. Sold many copies. Pot pourri of poems

1944. In hospital with his unit having moved on.

'I had no intention of losing contact with my section so next morning before six I rose and got my equipment together, filled my water bottle, acquired an American K Ration pack and sneaked out before it was light. Among old newspapers in the ward I had found a Telegraph containing a rather inadequate map of the route I hoped to take through Lisieux and Evreux as far as the immediate environs of Pacy-sur-Eure. Domiane was a few miles further on, on the road to Vernon. To passers-by I must have appeared as one of a lost legion with all my accoutrements tied or strapped haphazardly about me. I stumbled on through the misty avenues of the tree-lined highway, grimly determined to reach my destination before dusk that evening. My modes of transport were many and varied – an army truck, on the pillions of cycles and the confined space of a French truck bearing a fragrant load of Camembert cheese. Even so there was much walking to do although the new and changing scenery was delightful. Now utterly dejected after what had been wasted efforts I resolved either to camp under a tree for the night wrapped in my blanket or to seek shelter with a local farmer.'

'The road to Lisieux was pocked and pot holed and the verges were littered with the wrecks of war's tide. I was relieved to complete that part of the journey. A short distance beyond Lisieux at a forked road they dropped me as they were travelling in a different direction. I began to walk towards Evreux my equipment and kit harassing my every step. At length after I had walked a mile or so I rested against a battered German tank and watched the convoys pouring past in both directions. The great difficulty in hitch-hiking out here is picking out the vehicle which is not travelling in convoy, as convoyed vehicles are not allowed to stop. Eventually I thumbed another lift on a RCOS [Royal Corps of Signals] waggon and after that I had a sequence of short rides, first on a Canadian waggon and then on the pillions of Canadian and British motor cycles. As I wandered along, a Frenchman adorned in the usual cycling attire – beret, light checked jacket and wide plus fours pulled up when I bid him good day and I enquired if I was still traveling toward my next destination Evreux. He acquiesced and asked me for a cigarette. I gave him ten Players, and he told me he was from Paris and was travelling to Lisieux to stay with friends. He was seemingly very grateful for the cigarettes for he told me they were very hardly come by in Paris nowadays let alone anywhere else in France which I had visited. He left me and at about midday I sat on the verge of the road and ate part of the dinner unit from my American rations. I made short work of the tin of chopped ham and egg with biscuits and then finished up with four lumps of sugar to sweeten my mouth. To my dismay when I poured the water from my water bottle into my canteen it was the colour of red rust. So I had to dispense with that though my thirst rebelled against it. However, I eventually obtained a mug-full of cloudy well water. Walking on disparately thumbing vehicles that could not or would not stop, I caught sight of a French van chugging uncertainly up the hill behind me. It stopped. Here was my saviour indeed. 27 miles to Evreux! Was he going that far? Yes, he was! I bundled my surplus kit in the back of the vehicle and clambered into the cab, relief filling my breast. Although the aroma from the cheese was not too pleasant that could never deter me at such a moment. 20-18 kilometres read the sign posts and still we swayed precariously along. I thought that at any moment we would collapse in the centre of the road like a broody hen, stubborn, refusing to move an inch further. But no, we would make it yet. All the while I kept up a kind of conversation in pigeon French and the middle-aged cheese dealer appeared quite pleased that I could that I could speak a smattering of French. The chalk escarpments of Evreux hove in sight and there lay Evreux snuggly in the valley below. The Frenchman could take me no further. I thanked him and asked a Gendarme the direction to Domiane. He had never heard of it although I knew it lay only 8 kilometres away, or he may not have understood my pronunciation of the name. In Evreux, which, moreover, was barely touched by the ravages of war I made certain enquiries. A French child took me into a home where I was given a welcome draught of water followed by a large ripe pear whose juice ran appetisingly down my chin as I wandered towards Pacy-sur-Eure. I cursed under my breath the drivers who would not stop. It was only 7 kilometres ahead of me now. A cable truck took me the distance of three kilometres where I called in at a 2nd Army Signal dump. I asked them if they knew of the whereabouts of 10 Garrison Signals. No, they had never heard of such a section. From there I obtained a lift through Pacy-sur-Eure to where the road turns off to Domiane. I had now roughly two kilometres to go, my legs weak beneath me. When I had walked a kilometre a Captain and his batman-driver stopped and asked where I was heading for I must have looked the part of a lost member of the Foreign Legion. I informed him of whom I was searching and of my destination, and the he replied dashing all my hopes to the ground. 10 Garrison had moved off that morning to an unknown destination. But my story does not end there. The Captain who was in the Somerset Light Infantry advised me to return with him to camp, which lay just in the vicinity of Domiane, and to eat and sleep there the night, which I willingly did.

Richard does not record in this volume how he was reunited with his section. They continued through

Germany ending up at Potsdam. He had landed in Cherbourg on D plus 2 from Tilbury.